Maryland

MARYLAND BY ROAD

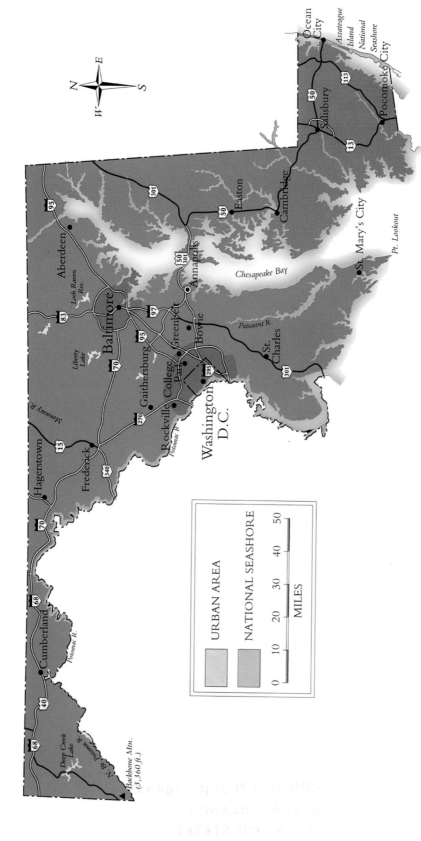

Ocean City
Assateague Island National Seashore
Pocomoke City
113
50
Salisbury
13
Cambridge
Easton
50
301
95
Aberdeen
Loch Raven Res.
501 301
Annapolis
Chesapeake Bay
St. Mary's City
Pt. Lookout
83
Baltimore
97
Greenbelt
Bowie
Patuxent R.
95
College Park
St. Charles
301
70
Liberty Lake
Gaithersburg
Rockville
270
295
Washington D.C.
Potomac R.
Monocacy R.
15
Hagerstown
Frederick
340
70
68
Cumberland
Potomac R.
40
68
Deep Creek Lake
N. Br. Potomac R.
Backbone Mtn. (3,360 ft.)

URBAN AREA

NATIONAL SEASHORE

0   10   20   30   40   50
MILES

Celebrate the States

Maryland

Leslie Pietrzyk and Martha Kneib

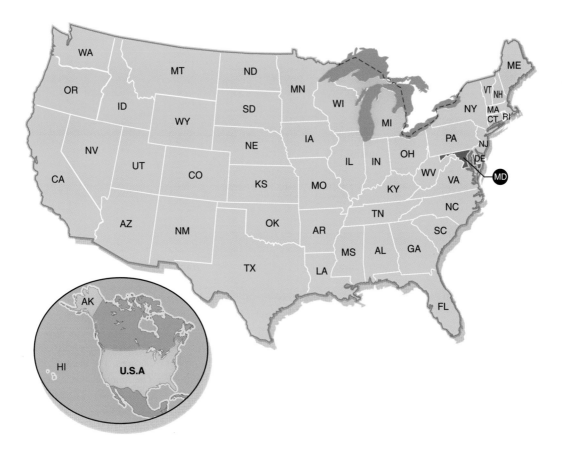

Marshall Cavendish
Benchmark
New York

Marshall Cavendish Benchmark
99 White Plains Road
Tarrytown, New York 10591-5502
www.marshallcavendish.us

All Internet sites were correct at time of printing.

Library of Congress Cataloging-in-Publication Data
Pietrzyk, Leslie, 1961-
Maryland / by Leslie Rauth and Martha Kneib. — 2nd ed.
p. cm. — (Celebrate the states)
Summary: "Provides comprehensive information on the geography, history,
wildlife, governmental structure, economy, cultural diversity, peoples,
religion, and landmarks of Maryland"—Provided by publisher.
Includes bibliographical references and index.
ISBN 978-0-7614-3004-9
1. Maryland—Juvenile literature. I. Kneib, Martha. II. Title.
F181.3.P54 2008
975.2—dc22
2007029497

Editor: Christine Florie
Contributing Editor: Nikki Bruno Clapper
Publisher: Michelle Bisson
Art Director: Anahid Hamparian
Series Designer: Adam Mietlowski

Photo research by Connie Gardner

Cover photo by Laurence Parent Photography

The photographs in this book are used by permission and through the courtesy of: *Alamy:* Philip
Scalia, back cover; *Photo Researchers, Inc.:* James L. Amos, 69; Jack Dermid, 29; *Viesti Associates Stock
Gallery:* 74; *Getty Images:* Greg Pease, 8, 97; Cameron Davidson, 13; Hulton Archive, 38, 46;
Stephen St. John, 59; Taylor S. Kennedy, 115 (B); Ron Vesely, 132; *Minden Pictures:* Gerry Ellis, 14;
Ross Nussbaumer/npl, 27; *Superstock Inc.:* Superstock, 12; Photographer's Choices, 19; Dean Fox,
92; *Dembinsky Photo Associates:* E.R. Degginger, 17; Bill Leaman, 115 (T); *The Image Works:* Roger
Viollet, 32; Andre Jenny, 100; Topham, 128; *Corbis:* Paul A. Souders, 11, 16, 21, 45, 67, 72, 84, 93,
105, 106, 112; Kevin Flemming, 15, 36, 86, 108, 125; David Muench, 23; Lowell Georgie, 35, 40;
c MAPS.com, 38; Bettmann, 42, 44, 49, 129; CORBIS, 48, 52, 53; Reuters, 55; James L. Amos, 56,
134; Micha Walter, 58; Annie Griffiths Belt, 65; Matthew Cavanaugh/epa, 78; Ross Pictures, 90;
Robert Kaufman, 103; Mark Abraham, 107; Gary W. Carter, 118; Nancy Kaszerman, 131;
NorthWind Picture Archives: 37, 39, 47; *Gibson Stock Photography:* 111.

Printed in Malaysia
1 3 5 6 4 2

Contents

Maryland Is . . .

Maryland is a land of vast beauty . . .

Maryland "is bathed in a singular and various beauty, from the stately estuaries of the Chesapeake to the peaks of the Blue Ridge."

—writer H. L. Mencken, 1922

. . . and magnificent waters . . .

"This baye is the most delightfull water I ever saw."

—Father Andrew White upon arriving in Maryland in 1634

"The Chesapeake! . . . This was the magical place where the waters became wider than those of the Susquehanna, where storms of enormous magnitude churned up waves of frightening power. This was the river of rivers, where the fish wore precious shells."

—author James Michener

. . . which Marylanders appreciate deeply.

There has never been a more heightened sense of awareness, of urgency, about our environment, about our natural resources, about conservation, than there is right now in our country. But it is Maryland's role in America to be that middle state, that central state, that state around which the other states rally in times of great national challenge and adversity."

—Martin O'Malley, governor of Maryland

Maryland is filled with unexpected places . . .

"One Marylander's place is so different from another's. Maryland is no artful mosaic, no tapestry of fabrics carefully woven into a whole. It is more a kaleidoscope, bits and pieces thrown together."

—author Eugene L. Meyer

"Baltimore is a city of . . . neighbors sharing steamed crabs in the back yard, and downtown waitresses who call their customers Hon."

—newspaper columnist Michael Olesker

interesting people . . .

"When it comes to eating muskrat, that's when we separate real Eastern Shoremen from everyone else."

—Eastern Shore cook

"My ideal celebration would be sitting in the middle of the floor with a T-shirt on and a bushel of Baltimore crabs."

—Patti LaBelle

. . . and history.

"Ever since Mary Pickersgill sewed the very flag that inspired Francis Scott Key to pen the 'Star-Spangled Banner' in Baltimore in 1813, women have impacted the very fiber of Baltimore's cultural, artistic, and historic landscape."

—Leslie Doggett, president and CEO,
Baltimore Area Convention and Visitors Association

Maryland has some of everything—mountains, valleys, beaches, cities, suburbs, farms, and quiet country towns. Maryland started as a colony founded on religious tolerance. Today, its citizens come from all over the world. The spectacular Chesapeake Bay is only one of Maryland's many treasures. You might think you know Maryland, but this state will find ways to surprise you.

Chapter One
America in Miniature

Unforgettable. That's how many people describe Maryland, the state that's often called America in Miniature. Maryland's long history can be explored in places like Fort McHenry, the Concord Point Lighthouse, and the Piscataway Indian Museum. Its culture can be tasted in the many seafood restaurants that serve up authentic Maryland crab cakes, or heard in the accents of the "Bawlmers," or Baltimore natives. Whether you want to experience a sunrise on the Eastern Shore, participate in a clam-bake, enjoy a quiet hike in the mountains, or do all three, you can find what you're looking for in Maryland.

Maryland is bordered by Virginia and the District of Columbia to the south, West Virginia to the west, Pennsylvania to the north, and Delaware to the east. Thirty-one miles of Atlantic Ocean shoreline also form Maryland's eastern border. Maryland may be the forty-second largest state, but its vast array of plants, animals, and natural features make the state unique.

The Blue Ridge Mountains are known for their blue cast when seen from a distance.

THE MOUNTAINOUS WEST

The western counties of Maryland are very mountainous and covered with forest. According to journalist Eugene L. Meyer, it is "a land of splendid scenery, of Appalachian ridges and high meadows." The region's deep forests provide a pleasant retreat from more populated areas. "The mountains are aflame in autumn and serene in summer," Meyer once wrote.

The state's highest point is in this region. Backbone Mountain, in the Allegheny Mountains, is 3,360 feet high. The narrowest part of the state is also located in western Maryland. In the town of Hancock, you can cross the state by traveling only 2 miles.

East of the Allegheny Mountains is a series of valleys with fertile soil. Farmers grow grain on picturesque farms, and there are a lot of apple orchards. Marble and limestone come from this region. Here workers quarried the marble that was used to build most of the Washington Monument in Washington, D.C.

Farther east rise the Blue Ridge Mountains. This is one of the loveliest areas of Maryland, where waves of forested mountains meet the sky. On bright days, a blue haze seems to hover in the distance. This haze gives the mountains their name.

PIEDMONT PLATEAU

Past the mountains, the land slopes into a series of rolling hills called the Piedmont Plateau. Farms growing wheat, corn, oats, and other crops dot the landscape. Horse farms are also common in the Piedmont. Breeders here raise twice as many Thoroughbred horses per square mile as breeders in Kentucky do.

The Piedmont Plateau comes to a dramatic end. The altitude drops, and the rivers that flow gently through the hills suddenly cascade to the

Great Falls is one of the highlights of the Potomac River.

plains below in several waterfalls. This point, where the Piedmont Plateau ends and the Atlantic Coastal Plain begins, is called the Fall Line. Historically, boats could not travel any farther up the river than the Fall Line. This is where settlers built the town of Baltimore.

One of the Fall Line's most remarkable waterfalls is Great Falls on the Potomac River. Only 15 miles northwest of Washington, D.C., this raging white water is a popular site for picnickers and hikers escaping the city for an afternoon.

ATLANTIC COASTAL PLAIN

More than half of Maryland is part of the Atlantic Coastal Plain, which stretches from New Jersey to Florida. The Chesapeake Bay cuts Maryland's portion of the plain into two sections: the low-lying Eastern Shore and the higher ground of the Western Shore. The Eastern Shore is a part of a peninsula shared by three states—Delaware, Maryland, and Virginia—which is sometimes referred to as the Delmarva Peninsula.

The Eastern Shore is filled with marshy wetlands. The sky looms high overhead; few trees break up the flatness. Produce and poultry farms stretch out alongside roads, and every back road seems to lead to a marsh, a creek, the bay, or the ocean. The Western Shore is similar but more forested.

These Eastern Shore wetlands are on the Little Choptank River, a tidal estuary of the Chesapeake Bay.

RIVERS

Most of Maryland's rivers flow into the Chesapeake Bay. The Potomac, Maryland's longest river, winds for 285 miles along the state's southern border before spilling into the bay. The East Coast's biggest river is the Susquehanna, which starts in New York, travels through Pennsylvania and Maryland, and then empties into the Chesapeake Bay. Other important rivers on the Western Shore are the Severn, the Gunpowder, the Patapsco, and the Patuxent. On the Eastern Shore, the Chester, Nanticoke, Choptank, and Pocomoke rivers flow into the bay.

The Maryland General Assembly designated a 21-mile segment of western Maryland's Youghiogheny River (known as the Yock) as Maryland's first Wild River. Thanks to the Yock's remote and rugged character, some threatened or endangered plants and animals that are no longer found elsewhere still survive there. To maintain the river's unique beauty, logging and development are limited around the Yock. The area is ideal for trout fishing, white-water rafting, and hiking.

The Potomac is the fourth-longest river system on the Atlantic Coast.

PLANTS AND ANIMALS

About 30 percent of Maryland is covered with trees. Most of the forests are found in western Maryland on the Piedmont Plateau. Spruce, hemlock, white pine, maple, and hickory trees are particularly plentiful. Yellow pine, cedar, and red gum trees grow in southern Maryland. The wetlands along the Chesapeake Bay have cypress trees. The oldest tree in Maryland, which toppled in 2002 after a violent thunderstorm, was said to be the Wye Oak in Talbot County. The tree measured 31 feet around and lived to be more than 450 years old.

Eighty-four species of mammals, 233 species of birds, 85 species of amphibians and reptiles, and 116 species of fish live in Maryland, along with thousands of species of insects, crustaceans, spiders, worms, and other creatures. Deer abound throughout the state. Red and gray foxes, raccoons, squirrels, opossums, skunks, woodchucks, weasels, and

The red fox's natural range is worldwide. The species is native to Europe, North America, North Africa, and Asia, including the islands of Japan.

cottontail rabbits live in the forests. A few bears remain in the mountainous regions of the state. The Delmarva fox squirrel, an endangered species, lives on the Eastern Shore.

Wild ponies roam Assateague Island, a barrier island in the Atlantic Ocean. Legend has it that the ponies are descended from a sixteenth-century herd that swam ashore from a sinking Spanish ship. Most likely, however, the ponies escaped from domesticated herds that grazed on the island.

Wild ponies run on the beach on Assateague Island.

Many species of birds live in or migrate through Maryland every year. Bird spotters have observed forty-one types of ducks, including mallards, black ducks, canvasbacks, wood ducks, and northern pintails. Birds that winter in Maryland include Canada geese, snow geese, and tundra swans. Shorebirds such as great blue herons, sandpipers, plovers, gulls, and terns also live in Maryland.

A great blue heron sits on a tree stump at Blackwater National Wildlife Refuge.

Away from the water, Marylanders enjoy watching cardinals, bluebirds, wrens, doves, mockingbirds, and many other types of songbirds. Hawks soar overhead. The state has several nesting areas for bald eagles, including the Blackwater National Wildlife Refuge and Calvert Cliffs State Park. The state bird is the Baltimore oriole, named after Lord Baltimore. This historic figure chose orange and black as the colors of his coat of arms because he admired the vibrant bird.

The Chesapeake Bay is filled with many varieties of fish, such as the alewife, the Atlantic needlefish, the Eastern silvery minnow, and the mummichog. The bay is even better known for its shellfish. In fact, the word *Chesapeake* comes from a Native American word meaning "great shellfish bay." Maryland is so proud of its reputation as a source of shellfish that it even has an official state crustacean—the Maryland blue crab. Maryland writer Tom Horton once remarked, "We love our crabs in Chesapeake country—love to eat them steamed and fried, in crab cakes and

The Maryland blue crab was designated Maryland's state crustacean in 1989.

stuffed into flounder and striped bass fillets." The Chesapeake provides 50 percent of the nation's blue crab harvest.

The bay also supports a wide variety of plant life, including redhead grass and eelgrass. Both of these species are important food sources for waterfowl. Eelgrass is the only true sea grass (grass that grows in salt water) found in the Chesapeake Bay area. Because eelgrass thrives in cold water, it grows best in spring and autumn and dies back in summer unlike most other plants in the region. Juvenile blue crabs use the grass for protective cover, as do small fish and seahorses.

CLIMATE

Like many other aspects of Maryland, the state's climate has a little bit of everything. Eastern Maryland enjoys mild winters, although the summers can be quite warm and humid. Western Maryland is generally 15 to 20 degrees Fahrenheit colder than the eastern areas, which are closer to sea level. The average mean temperature in the mountainous western part of the state is 48 °F. Near the Chesapeake Bay, the average mean temperature is 58 °F. Garrett County has an average annual snowfall of 100 inches, compared to just 8 to 10 inches on the Eastern Shore.

Summers in the mountains are delightfully cool. In the higher elevations, the temperature tops 90° F on an average of only two to ten days per year. Along the coast, this number rises to fifteen to twenty-five days per year. In the central portion of the state, away from both the mountains and the sea, between thirty and forty days per year will be over 90° F.

Occasionally, hurricanes or small tornadoes hit Maryland. In general, however, nothing worse than a thunderstorm or a snowstorm strikes the state.

A DELICATE BALANCE

"The Bay. There is no possible confusion with any other body of water, no need for more precise description," wrote William W. Warner in his award-winning book *Beautiful Swimmers*. Indeed, nothing defines Maryland like the Chesapeake Bay. It's what people think of first when they think of the state.

While the entire bay is only 200 miles long, it has 4,000 miles of shoreline in Maryland. At first glance the bay may not seem very dramatic. Tom Horton wrote, "Physically, the Chesapeake estuary is among the gentlest bodies of water of its size, lacking furious currents, rocky shoals, mammoth waves, or even much of a daily tidal drop." It's the special combination of all the bay's parts that makes it so beloved by Marylanders. In Baltimore's busy Inner Harbor, which is located in the tidal area of the Patapsco River before it empties into the bay, people step aside from the bustle to stare down at the rippling water, to gaze out beyond the lights, and to ponder where those ripples could carry them. The same bay also includes a series of intricate Eastern Shore creeks and marshes clogged with thick grasses. There, the only sounds are birds calling to one another and the lapping of gently moving water.

When Marylander Cindy Herrle talks about the Chesapeake Bay, she seems to be describing a person: "The bay has multiple personalities—some days it's very calm and peaceful, and some days it's very angry. When it's angry, whitecaps crowd the surface, and waves can reach 5 or 6 feet. It's fairly moody. Some days the water is flat and calm in the morning, by afternoon it's rough, and then by evening, everything's all smoothed out again."

An aerial view of the Chesapeake Bay

The Chesapeake Bay formed at the end of the last ice age, between 12,000 and 18,000 years ago. As glaciers retreated and the polar ice caps melted, sea levels began to rise. The rising ocean engulfed the east coast of North America. It flooded the Susquehanna River valley and created the bay. Today, the Chesapeake's average depth is only 21 feet, though its deepest point is 170 feet.

Maryland's top environmental concern is the health of the Chesapeake Bay. It is the nation's largest estuary—a combination of salty ocean water and freshwater from rivers, tides, and rain. Only a delicate balance can sustain the 2,700 species of oysters, crabs, fish, and other organisms that call the bay home.

LAND AND WATER

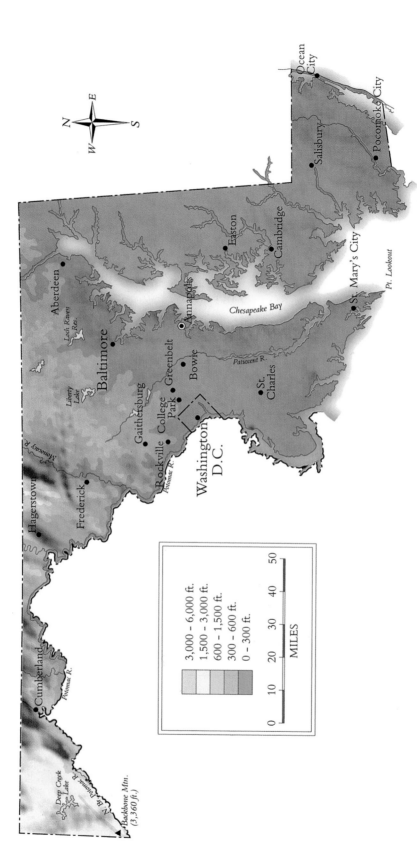

For at least twenty years, Marylanders have realized that their bay is in trouble. Pollution has been taking its toll. Rivers that feed into the bay pass through areas with many farms. Fertilizer and nutrient-rich manure produced by cattle end up in the rivers, which flow into the bay. Too many nutrients upset the bay's delicate balance. Certain organisms, such as floating algae, thrive on these fertilizers and nutrients. The growing population of algae blocks out light and oxygen crucial to the survival of underwater plants. In turn, water birds have fewer plants to eat, and crabs have nowhere to hide.

Smoke pollutes the air along the Chesapeake Bay at a steel plant in Baltimore.

PFIESTERIA HYSTERIA

In the autumn of 1996, fishermen along the Pocomoke River noticed something alarming. They found several fish with lesions, or open sores, along their bodies. The following year, thousands of fish in this river died. Again, the fish had red sores on their bodies. Many people who handled these fish suddenly suffered short-term memory loss, nausea, rashes, and eye irritation. Exposure to the toxins through the air or water also caused the same symptoms in other people, such as water skiers and scientists working in the field.

Scientists discovered that the fish were afflicted by *Pfiesteria piscicida*, a toxic microbe that normally feeds on bacteria or algae but sometimes attacks fish. No one truly understands why or when the microbe changes its diet. *Pfiesteria* has been identified in several rivers and creeks around the Chesapeake Bay. It probably lives in many other bays as well.

Once the health threat was established, Maryland governor Parris Glendening quickly closed the Pocomoke River to swimming, fishing, and boating. He also asked a commission of experts to study the problem. The governor's decision was controversial. Many people thought he was overreacting and alarming people needlessly. Sales of Maryland seafood plummeted, even though eating *Pfiesteria* has never been shown to cause people any problems. The governor stood his ground, however. He said, "We could not delay the announcement of the health risk." Today, the microbe is less of a problem. However, the state is still working to solve this vexing problem. Little has been learned about the organism.

You can lessen your chances of exposure to toxins by avoiding bodies of water that the state has closed to public use. Also avoid contact with sick fish. If you happen to find a fish with lesions on it, you can report it to the Maryland Department of Natural Resources Fish Health Hotline. If you call, be prepared to report the following information: the species of the fish; the date, time, and location where it was caught or found; and any sores or injuries you noticed.

CHESAPEAKE WHITE GOLD

The native oyster of the Chesapeake Bay, *Crassostrea virginica*, was once the linchpin in a state industry. It was also vital to the health of the bay. Old timers referred to the oysters as white gold because they were so valuable. Toward the end of the twentieth century, however, Maryland's oyster industry was deeply troubled. A decline in the water quality of Chesapeake Bay, as well as disease, had caused many oysters to die off. Eventually, oysters had to be imported from outside Maryland to satisfy the demand.

Oysters became so important to the economy that Marylanders started calling them white gold.

In 2005, Maryland's oyster harvest stood at 25,000 bushels. This was hardly a drop compared to the 2.5 million-bushel harvests of the 1970s. Today, oyster populations are only 1 percent of what they were even a century ago.

Marylanders do not intend to see their oysters—or their oyster industry—disappear without a fight. Oysters are not only an important part of Maryland culture, but also an essential component of the Chesapeake Bay's ecosystem. Oysters help maintain the bay's delicate environmental balance by filtering out excess algae and silt as they take water through their bodies. At one time, there were enough oysters to filter the water of the entire bay every week or two. Now it takes nearly a year. It's essential for the health of Chesapeake Bay that oysters return to their former numbers.

In an effort to rebuild the oyster population, state officials placed restrictions on how many oysters can be harvested. Baby oysters are being grown in hatcheries and then introduced into the bay. Native bay grasses are being replanted to help restore the habitat to its natural state. John R. Griffin, secretary of the Maryland Department of Natural Resources, said, "Critical to our success in increasing the Bay's oyster population will be ensuring our efforts are science based and action-oriented, and will not pose a threat to our fragile ecosystem."

So far, the tens of millions of dollars spent and the great effort of many people have not resulted in great gains. Oysters are showing some short-term population gains in limited areas, but overall, the bay itself is still in trouble. Silt continues to dump into the bay and to cover live oyster beds. The diseases Dermo and MSX, which have spread to over 90 percent of the bay, will remain a problem in the foreseeable future.

OYSTER DISEASES

Both Dermo and MSX are diseases caused by protozoans—one-celled organisms. The protozoan that causes Dermo is called *Perkinus marinus*, and the organism that causes MSX is *Haplosporidium nelsoni*. Both organisms prefer warm water, and therefore summer is the main season when infections occur.

MSX first invades the oyster's gills and then spreads to the rest of its tissues. Scientists don't yet know exactly why oysters die from MSX, but the probable cause is poor respiration, or breathing. The parasite that causes Dermo enters the oyster's digestive system after the oyster eats it. Oysters die from blocked blood vessels or tissue lysis (the breakdown of cell membranes).

Scientists have limited understanding of the two protozoans. They don't know how to cure or to control the spread of either Dermo or MSX. Fortunately, neither of these protozoans is harmful to people. Therefore, a person can eat an infected oyster without risk.

The future looks so poor for Maryland's native oysters that some people have suggested introducing an Asian species, *Crassostrea ariakensis*, into the bay. This oyster is larger than the native oyster, grows quickly, and might be resistant to common diseases. If introduced into the Chesapeake, the Asian oyster could take up the native oyster's job of filtering the bay's water, thereby increasing water clarity and oxygen levels. Other species, such as bay grasses, might also begin thriving again.

On the downside, introducing species into areas where they have never lived before often has negative consequences. For example, gypsy moths were introduced to the United States in 1868. Within twenty years, they had become a major pest. Every year, gypsy moth caterpillars remove the leaves of trees on over 1,000,000 acres of the United States. Examples like the gypsy moth are warning signs that introducing species into a new area can cause serious complications that can be impossible to predict or to control. Thus, the proposal to put Asian oysters into Chesapeake Bay is something that everyone takes very seriously. No one knows if introducing a new oyster species will do more harm than good. To date, there is no definitive answer, and efforts to restock the bay with its native oyster continue.

OTHER THREATENED AND ENDANGERED SPECIES

There are more than three hundred rare, threatened, or endangered species in Maryland. One is the Bewick's wren *(Thryomanes bewickii)*. In the nineteenth century, naturalist Robert Ridgeway noted that the Bewick's wren "is found about the cowshed and barn; he investigates the pigsty; then explores the garden fence, and finally mounts to the roof and pours forth one of the sweetest songs that was ever heard."

This bird was once a common sight around towns and farms. Now only twenty pairs of Bewick's wrens are known to exist in Maryland, Virginia, and West Virginia combined. In some states, this bird is extinct. The Bewick's wren nests in small holes and eats insects. Female wrens lay five to eight eggs, which hatch after two weeks. After two more weeks, the young are ready to leave the nest.

The main reason that a species becomes endangered is the loss of its usual habitat, or place to live. Since Bewick's wrens are willing to live in the farmyard and the subdivision as well as the forest, however, the reason for

The endangered Bewick's wren can be distinguished from other wrens by its white-edged tail, white underbody, and rusty brown or grey unstreaked back.

their decline has been a mystery. One theory is that the house wren, a more aggressive species, has expanded its territory eastward and is taking away the Bewick's wren's food and nesting areas. Two other aggressive species introduced from Europe, the house sparrow and the starling, might also be partly responsible.

The Maryland Department of Natural Resources considers the plight of the Bewick's wren extremely important. Protection may have come too late, however. None of Maryland's pairs are known to be breeding.

A more hopeful fate may come to the Indiana bat *(Myotis sodalis)*. These bats are small—about 4 inches long with a wingspan of less than a foot. The bat is brown and has a pink or brown nose. Indiana bats, like some other bat species, are extremely helpful to humans. According to one estimate, a single bat can eat a thousand mosquitoes in an hour.

Indiana bats are in danger partly because they store just enough energy to get them through the winter. If the winter is especially long or if people wake them up during their hibernation, they can die of starvation before spring. Habitat loss also has led to the bats' decline.

A cluster of hibernating Indiana bats

In recent years, small numbers of Indiana bats have been returning to Maryland. The Maryland Natural Heritage Program encourages people to install bat houses on their property. The houses encourage more Indiana bats to return to the area.

Some of Maryland's native plant species are also endangered. For example, tawny cottongrass colonized Maryland after the last ice age ended. Today it lives in bogs (wetlands with acidic soil) up to 3,000 feet in elevation. As more and more of Maryland's wetlands are developed, tawny cottongrass is losing its habitat.

Tawny cottongrass is an endangered plant species in Maryland.

BUILDING YOUR OWN BAT HOUSE

Several species of bats, including endangered species like the Indiana bat, live in bat boxes provided by humans. To make a bat house, build a box about 2 feet tall and at least 14 inches wide. Provide a landing platform about 3 to 6 inches wide. Inside the box, install partitions so that the bats have several compartments to sleep in. Place the box at least 10 feet off the ground. The box should face the southeast or the southwest so that the sun can warm it during the day.

Use rough-sawn lumber for your bat box so that bats can cling to it. As its name suggests, rough-sawn lumber is rough to the touch. Most lumber you get at a lumber store will be rough-sawn. Also make sure the lumber is untreated. Many preservatives used in lumber can make bats sick or even kill them.

Many Web sites have instructions and diagrams for building your own bat box. Some Web sites and stores sell the boxes already made. Bats can make good neighbors!

The shale-barren ragwort is also endangered. This drought-resistant plant lives on southern-facing shale slopes in Washington and Allegany counties. These rocky slopes do not trap enough moisture to support trees or plants that need a lot of water. In the direct summer sun, the temperature on the ground in these rocky areas can reach 140 °F. To survive the lack of water and the high temperatures, shale-barren ragwort has a long, shallow root system and grows a multitude of white hairs to shade its stem and leaves.

THE FUTURE

In 1997, the federal and Maryland state governments agreed to pay Maryland farmers as much as $200 million to take 100,000 acres of farmland out of production and to plant trees and grasses as buffers against the pollution running into the Chesapeake Bay. Farmer Paul Crowl said, "It sounds like a good program—good for farmers and good for water quality." Studies show that forest buffers can remove some of the nutrients in the water that passes through them.

Overpopulation near the bay is also a problem. More than 2.3 million people live within 20 miles of the Chesapeake and its tributaries. Building houses near the water often destroys protective grasses, forests, and wetlands. "Managing growth is absolutely the toughest challenge we face," said an official with the Chesapeake Bay Foundation. Maryland has begun to restrict development along most of the remaining shoreline by requiring a 1,000-foot buffer zone around the bay and its tidal rivers. Maryland's Coastal Management Program prohibited construction on many flood plains of non-tidal streams and ponds, as well as on coastal flood plains. People keep coming, however. Several counties near the bay are among Maryland's fastest growing, and the impact of these new people remains to be seen.

A lot of work remains to be done to ensure the survival of the endangered species found in Maryland. Every year, as new people move into the state, its environmental problems become worse. Few of Maryland's conservation efforts have become runaway success stories. With more restrictions on growth, as well as environmental education programs, Marylanders might be able to reverse the trend.

Chapter Two

A Foundation of Tolerance

People first lived in Maryland about ten thousand years ago. Archaeologists have discovered the stone tips of spears used by these prehistoric men and women. Other evidence of early Americans includes petroglyphs (carvings on rock) and soapstone artifacts.

Petroglyphs can be found in many areas of the United States, but most of Maryland's have been destroyed over time. Native Americans carved the petroglyphs into the surfaces of soft rocks and then polished them with sand or a tool. According to legend, William Penn (1644–1718), the founder of Pennsylvania, asked Native Americans if they knew who had carved Maryland's petroglyphs. Few European settlers shared his interest in Native-American artwork, however. After a brief period of interest in the petroglyphs in the 1860s and 1870s, most people forgot about them. Many were destroyed to make way for new towns, roads, and dams.

Throughout Maryland's history, Baltimore's port has been a place of important arrivals and departures.

One destroyed site was called the Bald Friar site. When rising water levels behind a new dam threatened the petroglyphs there, the Maryland Academy of Sciences sent people to retrieve the petroglyphs by blasting them out with dynamite. The pieces that survived the explosion and rising waters are now all that remain of the site's original petroglyphs. The designs at Bald Friar consisted of sets of parallel lines, geometric shapes, concentric circles, and marks possibly depicting the sun. Another symbol is thought to be a face or a fish, but no one knows what message the carvers intended to communicate with the odd shape.

Maryland's only remaining petroglyph located in its original position is a carving on a rock face near Great Falls. The design consists of three concentric circles around three small pits. A small design resembling a tail sticks out of the top of the petroglyph. Since this petroglyph is near waterfalls, it has been suggested that it represents a fish. Stone fish weirs (traps) have been found in the area. This shows that the Native Americans depended upon the fish in the river to make up part of their diet. The petroglyph might have been a sign showing a place where fish were plentiful, or it might have been a petition to the spirits to keep the fish stocks healthy. Since the people who carved the Great Falls petroglyph are gone, we will never know.

At the northern end of Chesapeake Bay, in roughly 1300–1000 B.C.E., native peoples were mining soapstone to carve into bowls and other useful containers, beads, and pipes. Soapstone is a rock that is very soft and easy to carve. It often has a slippery texture, which is why it reminds people of soap. Today, archaeologists want to learn more about how the Native Americans quarried, carved, and distributed soapstone products. Currently, more than eight hundred soapstone artifacts have been found at about three hundred sites in Maryland and the District of Columbia.

These Native-American clay pipe bowls, found at St. Mary's City, are more than three hundred years old.

NATIVE AMERICANS

As time passed, the people living in the Maryland area developed into the nations that met the first colonists arriving from England. On the Eastern Shore were the Nanticoke, Choptank, Pocomoke, and Wicomico tribes. The Piscataway and Patuxent tribes lived on the Western Shore. These tribes all spoke Algonquian languages. To the north, where the Susquehanna River meets the Chesapeake Bay, lived the Susquehannock. This tribe sometimes attacked its more peaceful neighbors to the south.

A Nanticoke man wears traditional dress.

ALGONQUIAN CLOTHING AND LIFESTYLE

Many people assume that all Native Americans dressed alike and had similar customs, but that is not true. It was common for the natives of Maryland to let their hair grow very long, and many people had tattoos. Women dressed in knee-length skirts, and men wore breechcloths. People were not expected to cover themselves above the waist. In cold weather, men could attach pant legs to their breechcloths, and both men and women wore capes made of turkey feathers. Everyone wore moccasins on their feet, and many people wore jewelry. For special occasions, men and women painted their bodies. Some people wore one or two feathers connected to a headband.

The Chesapeake Bay region provided plenty of food for the Native Americans. Men hunted and trapped bears, deer, and wild turkeys. They hollowed out tree trunks to make canoes and went fishing with nets and spears. Women grew corn, beans, and squash and gathered clams, oysters, nuts, and strawberries. People lived in villages of wigwams, which were small round houses. Each village contained at least one food storage building and a council house for the leaders of the settlement to meet together.

In 1608, Englishman John Smith of the Jamestown settlement in Virginia sailed up the Chesapeake Bay and explored the region thoroughly. He went back to Virginia with the news that Maryland was a good place to settle, with many opportunities for trading tools and cloth in exchange for valuable furs from the Native Americans. Many men in Virginia believed Smith, and soon they were traveling to Maryland.

At that time, many of the Algonquian-speaking tribes of Virginia and the eastern Chesapeake Bay had come together under the leadership of Wahunsonacock, who was called Powhatan by the English settlers. This alliance was called the Powhatan Confederacy. It included many different groups, including the Pamunkey, Mattapony, and Chickahominy. They lived in two hundred settlements, many protected with palisades (tall wooden fences). Although at first the English seized some of the confederacy's land, the area was peaceful for a time. In 1609, Christopher Newport gave Powhatan a crown and a coronation ceremony. Powhatan's daughter, Matoaka, married Englishman John Rolfe in 1614. Matoaka is better known by her nickname, Pocahontas.

John Smith (1580–1631) was one of the first European explorers to investigate the Chesapeake Bay area.

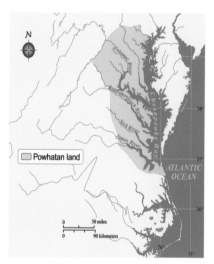

Powhatan's tribal lands were located on the East Coast from Maryland to Virginia.

By 1618, however, Powhatan and his daughter had died. Powhatan's successor, Opechancanough, orchestrated an attack on the English settlers and killed 350 of them. Retaliations on both sides continued for years. In 1644, Opechancanough was captured, taken to Jamestown, and murdered. His loss weakened the confederacy. By 1722, the native tribes that once had controlled much of the Chesapeake Bay area were scattered.

LORD BALTIMORE'S DREAM

Meanwhile, in England, Sir George Calvert asked King Charles I to give him land to found a colony in Maryland. Calvert, who was the lord of the English province of Baltimore, did not belong to the Church of England as most of the British did. He was Roman Catholic. At that time, the practice of Catholicism was illegal in England. Calvert's dream was to found a colony in the New World where people of different religious faiths could live together in peace. King Charles agreed to Calvert's request in 1632—two months after Calvert had died. Eventually, the king granted the official charter to Calvert's son, Cecil, Second Lord Baltimore.

Cecil Calvert, Second Lord Baltimore, received a charter to found the colony of Maryland from King Charles I of England in 1632.

In 1634, two ships, the *Ark* and the *Dove*, brought about 150 people, both Protestant and Catholic, to the new land. The colonists reached St. Clement's Island on the Potomac River, and on March 25, 1634, the priests traveling with them held the first-ever Catholic mass in Maryland. After several weeks of exploring, the newcomers found a small inlet on the western side of the bay.

They wanted to settle there but found that the Yaocomico Native Americans were already in the area. However, the Yaocomico were in the process of evacuating the area due to raids by their enemies, the Susquehannock. The settlers gave the Yaocomico cloth, axes, hatchets, and farm tools in exchange for their houses and moved directly into the village. Before moving on to a new location later that spring, the Yaocomico taught the settlers agricultural techniques.

The new Marylanders started farming their lands with wheat, corn, and tobacco. Tobacco was especially profitable, and soon farmers established tobacco plantations—huge, family-owned estates that required many workers. At first this work was done by indentured servants, poor people, and prisoners whose passage from England to Maryland had been paid for by wealthy colonists. In return, the indentured servants were required to

Tobacco was an important crop in Maryland during the seventeenth century. This tobacco note is from 1685.

work four years or more. By 1700, however, enslaved Africans were working the plantations.

More and more colonists were coming to Maryland and taking over land that had been used by the Native Americans. Some of the tribes fought to keep their lands, but they couldn't win. European diseases such as smallpox took a toll on the native population. The once-mighty Susquehannock were pushed from place to place. In 1763, a Pennsylvania mob murdered the last twenty members of the tribe. Today, only about half of Maryland's small Native-American population is descended from the region's original tribes. The others are descendants of tribes that came to Maryland from other places after colonial times.

FIGHTING A WAR

During the eighteenth century, a border dispute raged between Pennsylvania and Maryland. Two surveyors were hired to settle the matter. Charles Mason and Jeremiah Dixon completed their work in 1767, and the line they drew became known as the Mason-Dixon Line. This border not only separates Maryland from Pennsylvania but also is considered the dividing line between the North and the South.

In 1775, war broke out between the United States and Great Britain. More than 23,000 Marylanders fought in the American Revolution. During the Battle of Long Island, Maryland soldiers proved their bravery

Mason and Dixon established the Mason-Dixon Line between 1763 and 1767.

by holding off the British so that other American troops could make their way to safety. General George Washington said, "No troops poured out their blood more freely for the common cause than those of Maryland." Those Maryland soldiers, whom Washington called "troops of the line," gave Maryland one of its nicknames—the Old Line State.

The official end of the Revolutionary War came in January 1784, when the Treaty of Paris was ratified in Annapolis at the Maryland State House. Maryland became the seventh state of the new country four years later when it ratified the U.S. Constitution. In 1791, Maryland (along with Virginia) donated land on the Potomac River to the young nation for the building of a permanent capital city—Washington, D.C.

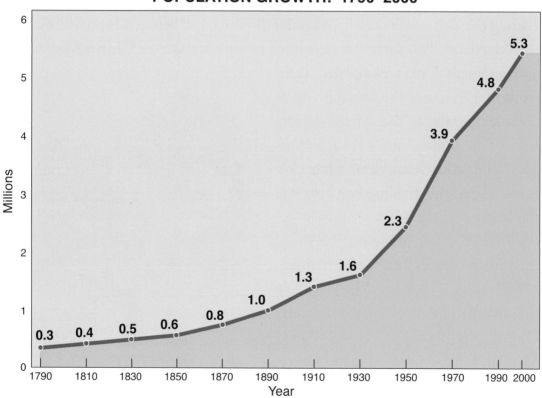

POPULATION GROWTH: 1790–2000

BUILDING A NEW COUNTRY

By this time Baltimore had become Maryland's major port and the largest city south of the Mason-Dixon Line. In the whole country, only the cities of New York, Philadelphia, and Boston were larger. It seemed that the United States was off to a fine beginning, as trade with many other countries was strong. Also, since the United States was officially neutral in the ongoing war between Britain and France, U.S. merchants had been making lots of money selling goods to both sides. British and French ships sailed in danger of being attacked, and the loss of merchant ships hurt both countries. However, American ships sailed without interference and thus could take advantage of trade routes that the British and French were no longer using.

The British accused the Americans of being allies of the French, and captains began seizing American sailors to serve on British ships. The British had used this custom, called impressment, to man their own ships for four hundred years. The practice infuriated the U.S. government and, along with other issues, caused U.S. president James Madison to declare war.

Maryland played a central role in the War of 1812. The British wanted to capture the port of Baltimore because it was an important trade center. In 1814, British ships attacked Fort McHenry in the Battle of Baltimore. James Ellicott, who observed the scene, wrote, "The bombardment of the fort was a scene interesting; terrible and grand. During the whole of last night we were able from the tops of the houses in town to trace every rocket and shell from the time it left the mortar until it struck or exploded in the air."

Another Marylander watching this attack was Francis Scott Key, who was arranging for the release of a prisoner on a British ship in the harbor. As the British shot more and more ammunition, the sky filled with smoke. As night fell and the smoke thickened, Key could no longer see the American flag above Fort McHenry. The next morning, when he saw

Francis Scott Key gestures to the American flag as Fort McHenry is bombarded.

the American flag still waving high above the fort, he scribbled words of relief on the back of an envelope. These words were the poem that became "The Star-Spangled Banner," the national anthem of the United States.

After the war ended, the country turned to solving other problems, including improving transportation. In 1824, work began on the Chesapeake and Delaware Canal, a waterway that provided ships a shortcut between Baltimore and the Atlantic Ocean. In 1828, construction started on the Chesapeake and Ohio Canal in an effort to link Washington, D.C., and the Potomac River with the Ohio River valley. Although the canal was never finished, it reached western Maryland in 1850.

The Chesapeake and Ohio Canal is a peaceful sight at the C&O Canal National Historical Park.

Even more important than the canals was the railroad. In 1830, the Baltimore and Ohio Railroad began offering the nation's first passenger rail service between Ellicotts' Mills and Baltimore. The steam-powered locomotives traveled at 20 miles per hour—unheard of at the time!

Officials lay the first stone of the Baltimore and Ohio Railroad.

A DIVIDED NATION

As the young country grew, people's views regarding slavery began to change. While slavery was declared illegal in all the Northern states in 1804, the Southern states refused to yield to pressure to outlaw slavery. Maryland was in the middle of this increasingly bitter fight. Baltimorean McHenry Howard wrote to a friend, "I live just between the North and the South, hearing both sides of the question and *feeling* both sides."

In April 1861, Southern states began seceding (separating) from the Union. They formed the Confederate States of America. Maryland was located south of the Mason-Dixon Line, but it did not secede. President Abraham Lincoln sent Union troops into Maryland to prevent secession because he did not want Washington, D.C., to be totally surrounded by Confederate states and thus cut off from the North. War broke out in South Carolina on April 12.

Some Marylanders were still torn about which side to support. Many farmers in western Maryland and the Piedmont did not favor slavery. On the other hand, the tobacco planters in southern Maryland wanted slaves to work on their big plantations. Historians estimate that 20,000 Marylanders joined the Confederate army during the course of the war, and in many areas—particularly southern Maryland and the Eastern Shore—citizens sided with the South. Many Marylanders who fought for the Union joined regiments dedicated to guarding Maryland rather than to invading the South. Approximately 25,000 Maryland men joined the Union army, and an additional 5,000 served as Union sailors and marines.

Pictured here is a banner commemorating the secession convention in Charleston, South Carolina, in 1861. Maryland attended the convention but eventually did not secede.

THE UNDERGROUND RAILROAD'S GREATEST CONDUCTOR

During the nineteenth century, many people decided that they could not sit by idly and tolerate slavery. The Underground Railroad helped slaves make their way to safety and freedom in the North and Canada by following a route of safe havens. Free African Americans and sympathetic whites guided the runaway slaves from one place to the next, at great risk to their own safety.

Harriet Tubman, who was born into slavery on an Eastern Shore Maryland plantation, was one of the most famous "conductors" of the Underground Railroad. When she was almost thirty years old, she escaped to the North with the help of the Underground Railroad. It was a slow, house-to-house journey from Maryland to Delaware to freedom in Pennsylvania. She said, "When I found I had crossed that [Mason-Dixon] line . . . the sun came like gold through the trees, and over the fields, and I felt like I was in Heaven." Tubman vowed she would return for the people she had left behind. She returned to Maryland many times to lead slaves to freedom. She said, "On my Underground Railroad I never ran my train off the track and I never lost a passenger."

At one point, plantation owners offered a $40,000 reward for Tubman's capture—far more than the fees of $25 to $150 that were normal for returning a runaway slave. Thanks to Tubman's heroism, members of her family—as well as many others—were able to live the rest of their lives in freedom.

The Battle of Antietam, which took place on September 17, 1862, was the bloodiest one-day battle in American history.

Maryland was the site of one of the worst battles in the Civil War (1861–1865). The Battle of Antietam was fought in 1862. More than 23,000 Union and Confederate soldiers were killed in a single day near Sharpsburg in western Maryland. James H. Rigby, a Confederate soldier, described the battle: "The crying of the wounded for water, the shrieks of the dying, mingled with the screeching of the shells, made up a scene so truly appalling and horrible that I hoped to God, that I might never witness such another."

The Civil War ended on April 9, 1865. Five days later, Marylander John Wilkes Booth killed President Lincoln in Washington, D.C. Booth escaped to Maryland and later was caught in Virginia.

MARYLAND GROWS

After the war, Baltimore grew rapidly. Its population nearly doubled from 267,354 to 508,957 between 1870 and 1900. New Baltimoreans came from rural parts of the United States and from many European nations, including Germany, Ireland, Russia, and Poland.

BALTIMORE FIRE

On February 7 and 8, 1904, a tremendous fire wiped out a large section of downtown Baltimore. Jones Falls, referred to in the song as "silver falls," was one of the points at which the blaze began to retreat.

It was on a sil-ver falls by a nar-row That I
Then a - mid an aw-ful scene of com-mo - tion, The—

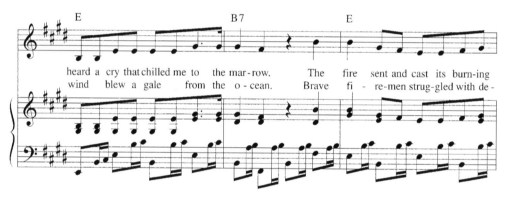

heard a cry that chilled me to the mar-row. The fire sent and cast its burn-ing
wind blew a gale from the o - cean. Brave fi - re-men strug-gled with de -

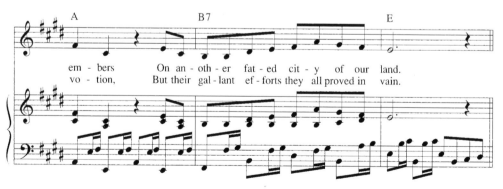

em - bers On an - oth - er fat - ed cit - y of our land.
vo - tion, But their gal - lant ef - forts they all proved in vain.

Fire,   fire,   I heard the cry,   From ev - 'ry breeze. that
Strong   men   in an - guish prayed,   Call - ing out— to

passed me by.   All   the world— was   one sad cry of—
heav'n for aid,   While   the fire— in   ru - in laid Fair—

pi - ty,—   Bal - ti - more, the beau - ti - ful   cit - y.—

In 1917, the United States entered World War I (1914–1918), and more than 60,000 Marylanders served in the military. Maryland's workers contributed to the war effort by building ships and producing such necessities as canned food. After the war, Maryland's economy continued to grow until the Great Depression crippled the nation in the early 1930s. More than half of Maryland's factories closed or cut production during the Depression. World War II (1939–1945) lifted the country out of depression. Again, Maryland's factories contributed to the war effort with ships, nails, cargo planes, bombers, and more.

Female mechanics service an M-3 tank at Aberdeen Proving Ground in Harford County during World War II.

Back home, Maryland faced another challenging battle: the issue of civil rights, or equal treatment under the law for Americans of all races. In 1935, Donald Murray was prohibited from enrolling in the University of Maryland School of Law because he was black. Thurgood Marshall, an African-American lawyer, took the case to court and won. Murray became the first African-American student to enter a professional school at a state university south of the Mason-Dixon Line. That was just the beginning of a distinguished career for Thurgood Marshall, who eventually became the first African American to serve on the U.S. Supreme Court (from 1967 to 1991).

Left to right: Thurgood Marshall, Charles Houston, and Donald Gaines Murray prepare for a desegregation case against the University of Maryland in 1935.

In 1954, Baltimore's public schools were desegregated, and another battle was won.

Another face of Maryland was resurfacing after several centuries: the Native Americans. Since the early 1700s, native peoples had been living in scattered communities far from their ancestral lands. Some were in New Jersey; others were in Pennsylvania, Delaware, and Oklahoma. Still others had moved as far away as Canada. Many were descendants of both native and European ancestors. Their Algonquian languages had been lost. However, some dreamed of returning to their native ancestors' ancient homes and building native communities.

Many of the descendants of Powhatan had moved to New Jersey over time. In 1982, New Jersey agreed to cede 350 acres to the Powhatan Renape Nation; this land is now known as the Rankokus Indian Reservation. The reservation provides an administrative center that helps educate others about the cultural, social, and historic heritage of Powhatan's people.

Maryland has made some progress toward embracing its native peoples. The Piscataway Indian Museum in Brandywine has exhibits on the history and cultures of the Piscataway. It features a full-scale reproduction of a longhouse, the traditional dwelling of the Piscataway at the time of their contact with Europeans. The Piscataway have endured much since they first encountered Europeans in the early 1600s. However, as Dr. Gabrielle Tayac, niece of the Piscataway's hereditary chief, points out, "We are still here."

STILL AMERICA IN MINIATURE

As Maryland begins a new century, its people and places continue to reflect both the history and the future of the nation. In 2007, Governor Martin O'Malley signed a long-supported law requiring that government contractors pay their employees more than the minimum wage. This means

Maryland residents are benefiting from the nation's first statewide living wage law. Meanwhile, fans still flock to Baltimore for ball games at Camden Yards and hope for another Super Bowl win by the Ravens. Residents stroll along the peaceful C&O Canal. Government officials struggle to preserve the beauty of the Chesapeake. And thousands of Marylanders strive to solve worldwide problems as they work in the nation's capital.

MVP Ray Lewis celebrates the Ravens' victory over the New York Giants at Super Bowl XXXV in 2001.

Chapter Three

Diverse People

Maryland was founded as a colony of tolerance among Christians. This legacy is still alive today. Certainly Maryland is not problem-free, but overall, Marylanders today work even harder than their founders to understand and to accept others.

ETHNIC GROUPS

Before the Civil War, Maryland had the highest population of free African Americans of any state in the country. Religious and moral pressures had led many slave owners either to free their slaves outright or to grant them freedom in their wills. Many other African Americans were descended from early free blacks. Still others had bought their freedom from their owners.

In 1790, only one in thirteen blacks in Maryland was free. By 1810, that figure had risen to one in three. The 1860 census counted 84,000 "free people of color" in Maryland—25,000 more than the next-highest state. Free blacks lived primarily in Baltimore and on the Eastern Shore. They built their own communities and worked in a variety of careers, including farming, blacksmithing, and shop keeping.

A crewman works on an oyster boat.

Based on recent U.S. Census Bureau figures, African Americans constitute about 30 percent of Maryland's population. Prince George's County, just outside Washington, D.C., attracts many highly educated black professionals who wish to live in neighborhoods with other successful African Americans. In 2005, an estimated 62.7 percent of the county's residents were African American, and African Americans owned more than 30 percent of its businesses. Resident Clif Webb enjoys living there. He said, "Prince George's County has such a rich cultural and economic diversity that anyone's opportunities are only limited by his or her imagination."

Simmie Knox of Silver Spring was the first African American commissioned to paint a presidential portrait. His portraits of Bill and Hillary Clinton were unveiled at the White House in June 2004.

Large numbers of Asians and Latinos also call Maryland home. As of 2005, almost 5 percent of the state's population was Asian, and 5.7 percent was Latino (also called Hispanic). Maryland's Asian population is growing quickly. Between 2000 and 2005, the Asian populations of several counties, including Calvert, Carroll, Charles, Frederick, and Howard, increased by over 50 percent. By the mid-1990s, thirty-eight churches in Montgomery County were holding Korean-language services, and the area's first Vietnamese Catholic church had opened in the Baltimore area.

An Asian family has a happy moment in Baltimore.

ETHNIC MARYLAND

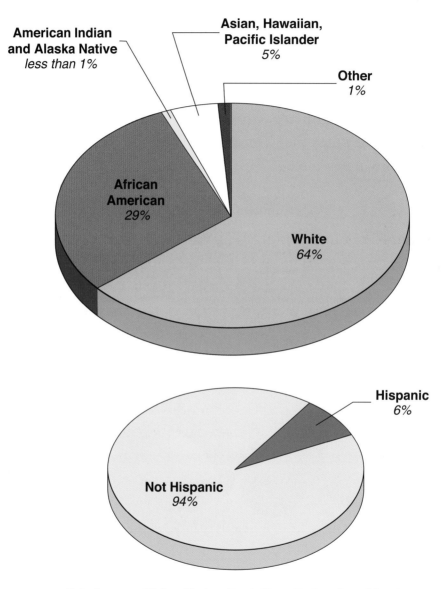

American Indian and Alaska Native
less than 1%

Asian, Hawaiian, Pacific Islander
5%

Other
1%

African American
29%

White
64%

Hispanic
6%

Not Hispanic
94%

Note: A person of Cuban, Mexican, Puerto Rican, South or Central American, or other Spanish culture or origin, regardless of race, is defined as Hispanic.

A few thousand Native Americans—about 0.1 percent of the total population—live in Maryland. There are also settlements of Amish, a religious group of people who do not rely on modern conveniences such as electricity.

Historically, Baltimore's Locust Point was second only to New York's Ellis Island as a point of entry for people coming by boat to the United States. Thousands of Irish people came to Maryland in the 1830s and 1840s, many of them to work on the Chesapeake and Ohio Canal. The 1850s brought coal miners from Wales. Thousands of Germans, Poles, Russians, and Italians also arrived during the 1800s. By 1870, one of every ten Marylanders was foreign-born.

Baltimore has been called a city of neighborhoods. Its nineteenth-century European immigrants tended to live near people from the same country so that they could speak their native language, find the foods they longed for, and help each other get jobs. Today, many of these neighborhoods maintain their ethnic flavor. "Fells Point is where I buy all my Polish kielbasa," said one suburban woman. "The Polish butcher shops are the best."

Baltimore celebrates its ethnic diversity with summer festivals that attract crowds seeking good food, music, and crafts. Among the heritages celebrated are Greek, Irish, Ukrainian, German, African American, Indian, Korean, Latino, and Polish. "I've been to the Polish festival at Patterson Park," said Baltimorean Melissa Berg. "It's a big outdoor party: polka bands and accordions, food you can't get anywhere else like three different versions of *bigos* [a stew, sometimes called the Polish national dish], breathtaking dancing. I'm proof that you don't have to be Polish to have fun at the festival!"

Maryland's recent immigrants make the state increasingly diverse. Many recent immigrants also live clustered together in ethnic neighborhoods.

"Lots of my neighbors are Filipino," said Veronica Puno, who moved from the Philippines to Prince George's County. "And most of the people go to my church. As much as we like it here in Maryland, we like to get together to talk about what's going on back 'home.'"

Some of Maryland's more recent immigrants have come from Cameroon. Conditions back home, including political unrest and poor economic opportunities, prompted many West Africans to seek better lives in the United States. People from Cameroon have settled in Hyattsville and Greenbelt in Prince George's County. During the 2006–2007 school year, 263 students from Cameroon were enrolled in the Prince George's County Public Schools. As recently as 1999, there were none. Although some of the immigrants plan to return to Cameroon someday, many plan to stay. Martha Ngwainmbi, a Cameroonian now living in Greenbelt, said, "Home is where you find peace of mind and comfort . . . once you are with your family—that's home."

A CROWDED STATE

More than 5.6 million people live in Maryland. That's a lot of people for such a small state. In Maryland, there is an average of 541.9 people per square mile. If you think that means a lot of people live in cities, you're absolutely right.

Much of Maryland is urban and suburban. Almost half the state's residents live in the metropolitan Baltimore area, and one-third live in suburban Washington, D.C. Western Maryland and the Eastern Shore are much less populated. More people are moving to the counties near the bay, however, to escape crowds, traffic, and other frustrations of urban living.

POPULATION DENSITY

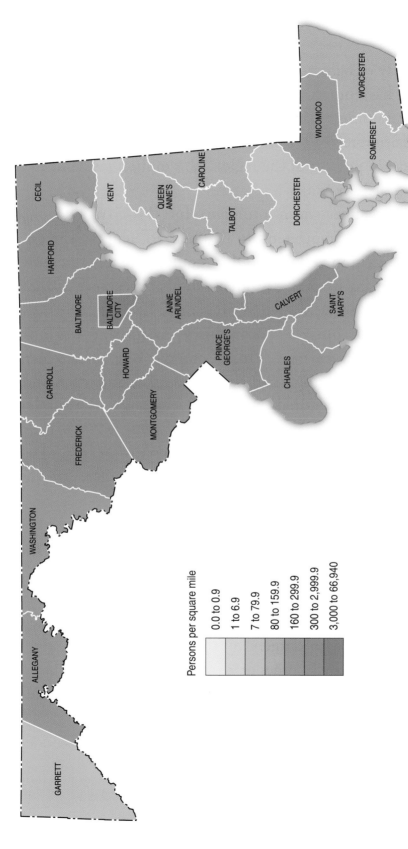

Persons per square mile

0.0 to 0.9
1 to 6.9
7 to 79.9
80 to 159.9
160 to 299.9
300 to 2,999.9
3,000 to 66,940

The city of Baltimore's population has decreased in recent decades, as people have moved to the suburbs and to the less urban counties. In 1950, Baltimore had 950,000 residents—71 percent of the people in the Baltimore region. In 2006, however, with only 631,366 residents, just 25 percent of the region's 2.5 million residents lived within the Baltimore city limits.

These changes mean problems for the city. The people who move out of Baltimore tend to be more affluent, so the poorer people are left behind. These people are unable to pay the same amount of taxes that the wealthier residents did, so it is more difficult for the city to pay for services such as police and fire departments and public schools. To compensate for this loss of tax revenue, lawmakers raised taxes on businesses. This discouraged businesses owners from staying in the city, too. The departure of middle-class and wealthy adults has also resulted in poorer children in Maryland's city schools. Some young people—at least 2,289 in 2005—are believed to be homeless or living in a shelter. Some of Maryland's homeless young people do not have enough to eat. Others are sleeping in abandoned buildings or on the street. Some of them may be able to stay with the families of friends for a few days here and there, but for the most part, these kids are on their own. Many of them make money through illegal activities.

Some kids are on their own because their parents have died. Others have parents in jail or parents who do not want them. They face the difficulties of survival largely by themselves. If found, the teens are placed in either foster homes or group homes. Since this means leaving their familiar neighborhoods and schools, however, most children do not want to be placed elsewhere.

A girl eats lunch at a day-care center for homeless families in Baltimore.

Part of the problem is that high-school age kids are too old to receive certain kinds of government benefits and too young to receive others. For instance, adults may receive housing subsidies, but teenagers cannot. In addition, shelters are often reluctant to accept teenage boys. Legal obstacles also stand in the way. Although a person as young as sixteen may sign a lease in Baltimore, it is illegal for anyone under eighteen to live without an adult guardian.

Marylanders have begun to notice this problem, and they are working to find solutions. Several legislators are backing changes in Baltimore's current foster-care policies. Nonprofit agencies such as Fellowship of Lights and Baltimore Homeless Services are also seeking changes. They want to set up dormitories where young people can go to eat, sleep, shower, and study. This will help homeless kids live safely in their own communities and finish high school. Without a high-school diploma, young people have few options open to them.

WHAT'S NEXT?

Maryland's local and state governments are working on innovative ways to ease the suffering of the state's cities and people. By expanding the Baltimore Convention Center, the city hopes to attract more visitors and investors. Additionally, Baltimore has special enterprise zones. Companies buying new properties or expanding their facilities in these areas receive enormous property tax benefits and other incentives. One local businesswoman said, "These zones help keep companies from moving out of Baltimore—taking jobs with them. Instead, they're willing to invest in property improvements and create jobs." Other residents object to the tax breaks because the extra money could be spent on social services or education.

Too few people is a problem, but so is too many people. Residents of Maryland's small towns and rural areas want to retain their charm while also taking advantage of economic opportunities that might bring in more people. "All of a sudden, everyone in this county seems to want to build a million houses," said Peggy Owens, a native of St. Mary's County in southern Maryland. "The good thing about living here was it was peaceful, quiet. You didn't have to worry about congestion and crime. Now, it's turning into a city, instead of country." Owens is talking about a trend called sprawl—the rapid, largely unplanned development of

The specter of suburban sprawl reaches northern Montgomery County.

homes and businesses in formerly rural areas. The Maryland Office of Planning works to lessen the negative impact of this trend.

LIFE ON THE EASTERN SHORE

Novelist Sophie Kerr once said, "If you have not had the luck to be born on the Eastern Shore you cannot know its people." The Eastern Shore is different from the rest of Maryland. Until the Chesapeake Bay Bridge was completed in 1952, the Eastern Shore was virtually inaccessible. People had to take ferries or drive all the way up around the bay to get there. Residents of the Eastern Shore felt isolated from the rest of the state. In fact, residents of the Eastern Shore tried five times to create their own state, separate from the rest of Maryland, most recently in the 1950s.

A WATERMAN'S TALL TALE

Here's a well-known tale told by watermen on the Eastern Shore:

Two Eastern Shore boys, Len and Ward, wanted to command their own ship. They'd been trained by one of the best watermen, Captain Tawes. But they were told, "You're too young. You can take the ship if Captain Tawes goes along too."

The boys begged Captain Tawes to come with them, and finally he agreed.

The three sailed down to the West Indies to load up fruit to bring back to Baltimore. The trip was going well until they got back to the bay and the fog set in so bad that every other ship anchored. But Len and Ward couldn't wait—it was a three-day fog for sure, and they didn't want the fruit to rot. Captain Tawes said, "We can do it, boys. Just bring me a sample from the bottom every half hour." Watermen claim they can tell exactly where they are by smelling the mud from the bottom of the bay.

So Len brought the first reading to Captain Tawes. He sniffed the mud and said, "Change your course about three points to the westward and that'll put you right in the middle of the channel."

Half an hour later, they brought more mud to Captain Tawes. He said, "Hold right on that course for the next half hour."

Back on deck, Ward said, "Does that old man know what he's saying?"

"Let's see," Len said.

They took dirt from a flowerpot that Len's mother, Betsy, had given him. They dunked the dirt in bay water, and Len took it down to Captain Tawes.

Captain Tawes looked at the mud, smelled it, looked again. "Quick, run and tell Ward to heave her hard to. You've run her right in the middle of Betsy's flower garden!"

This area of the state is home to a special type of Marylander: the Eastern Shore waterman. Watermen make their living off the Chesapeake Bay by catching crabs, oysters, clams, and fish. In some areas they are only allowed to use boats powered by wind when they go to work. The boats they use, called skipjacks, have one mast with triangular sails and a shallow, V-shaped bottom.

Their work is demanding and dangerous, with the constant risk of getting caught in a storm and drowning. Watermen go out in all sorts of weather—hot, cold, rainy, windy—and because they work for themselves, selling their catch to seafood distributors, there are no paid holidays for watermen.

Men on three skipjacks dredge oysters at dawn on the Chesapeake Bay.

CRAB CAKES

There are as many recipes for crab cakes as there are Marylanders. For a real Maryland flavor, add a pinch of Old Bay seasoning to the mayonnaise. Have an adult help you with this recipe:

1 pound lump crabmeat
1 cup crushed saltine crackers
1/2 cup mayonnaise
1 egg
1 tablespoon mustard
1 tablespoon Worcestershire sauce
tabasco sauce to taste

Preheat a broiler.

Spread the crabmeat out in a flat pan and sprinkle the crushed saltines over it. In a small bowl, mix the mayonnaise, egg, mustard, Worcestershire sauce, and Tabasco sauce. Pour this mixture over the crabmeat and gently mix everything together with your hands. Let the mixture sit for two to three minutes before forming the crab cakes.

Form the mixture into 8 mounded rounds about 3 inches across and 1 inch thick. Do not pack the crab too firmly—just enough to hold the shape.

Arrange the crab cakes on a buttered cookie sheet and broil them until they are heated through and slightly browned (about five to six minutes). Place aluminum foil over the crab cakes if they are browning too quickly.

Serve the crab cakes immediately.

Despite the risks, many watermen wouldn't dream of doing anything else. "When you're getting the oysters and the boat's going good and you've got a good crew, there's nothing like it," said waterman Wade Murphy. "You're out on the bay, and you're part of it."

Eastern Shore writer Gilbert Byron captured the spirit of the watermen in his poem "These Chesapeake Men":

> These men a sun-tanned, quiet breed
> With eyes of English blue and faces
> Lined with many a watch of sunlit waters . . .
> They seek the imperial shad and the lowly crab,
> The oyster, the weakfish, the turtle, the rockfish, . . .
>
> And food for their souls
> Which they sometimes find . . .
> In the setting of the sun
> In the quest of quiet harbor—
> In the Chesapeake.

AN UNUSUAL STATE SPORT

Maryland is one of six states to have a state sport. It's an unusual one—jousting! Jousting started in medieval times in Europe. Two armored knights on horseback carrying long lances would charge toward each other and try to knock their opponent off his horse. These tournaments were so dangerous that the Catholic church once threatened to withhold a Christian burial from anyone who died at one. King Henry II of England attempted to make them illegal because so many knights were getting injured. Jousting was too popular to be stopped, however,

Mark Virts, champion jouster, takes aim at a target during a competition in Port Republic.

and kings eventually gave up the idea of banning them. Instead, King Richard I of England taxed jousts for a new source of revenue!

Jousting in Maryland is a little less life-threatening. Jousters still ride horses and carry lances, but their goal is to get the lance through a small ring while riding at a gallop. In the first round, the rider tries three times to get three rings the size of a quarter onto the tip of his or her lance. If the rider gets all nine rings, he or she advances to the second round, where the rings are the size of a nickel. If the rider advances to the third round, the rings are even smaller—the size of a dime. The rings are hung on poles set 30 yards apart, and the rider has only nine seconds to complete the run. Taking too much time automatically results in being eliminated from the tournament.

The abilities of the horse and rider have to be well developed, or they will not do well in the competition. It takes at least two years of formal training before a horse is considered ready to enter jousting contests.

Today's jousting winners are chosen based on points scored, not bodies on the ground. Jousting in Maryland has its roots in the mid-nineteenth century, when young Maryland gentlemen took up the sport for its romantic appeal. Often tournaments concluded with a fancy ball and the crowning of a beautiful young lady as queen. Today, several societies in Maryland still host jousting tournaments.

Chapter Four

Strong in Deed, Gentle in Spirit

Maryland has had four constitutions over the course of its history. The first was adopted at the time of independence in 1776. Although originally about 8,800 words long, it was amended over the years until it reached 15,200 words. It allowed all Christians to worship without government interference and to hold positions in the government. In 1826, the document was amended to allow Jews to hold public office as well.

Eventually, an entirely new constitution was written and approved in 1851. Most of its changes focused on changing the voting districts for the Maryland General Assembly. During the Civil War, a third constitution was adopted. It outlawed slavery and banned Southern sympathizers from voting. After the war ended, this constitution was considered unworkable, and the fourth and present constitution was adopted in 1867.

Maryland's current constitution has been amended almost two hundred times. At 47,000 words, it is much longer than most state constitutions.

The heart of Maryland's government is the capitol in Annapolis.

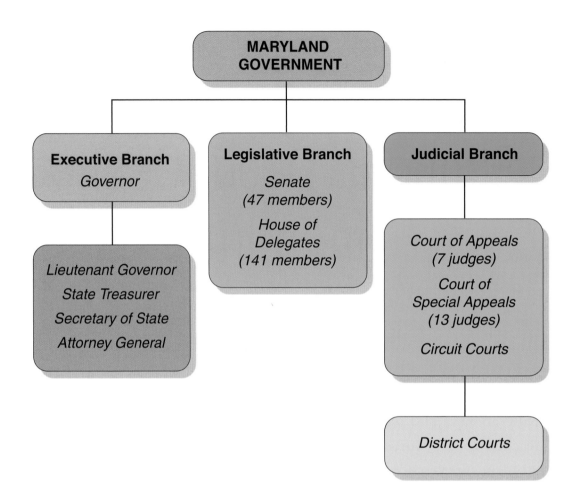

MARYLAND GOVERNMENT

Executive Branch
Governor

Lieutenant Governor
State Treasurer
Secretary of State
Attorney General

Legislative Branch
*Senate
(47 members)*

*House of
Delegates
(141 members)*

Judicial Branch

*Court of Appeals
(7 judges)*

*Court of
Special Appeals
(13 judges)*

Circuit Courts

District Courts

INSIDE GOVERNMENT

Like the federal government, Maryland's government is divided into three branches: executive, legislative, and judicial. A series of checks and balances ensures that no one branch becomes overly powerful.

Executive Branch

The executive branch implements and enforces Maryland's laws. The head of this branch—and of the state government as a whole—is the governor, who is elected to a four-year term. Among the governor's responsibilities are presenting the annual state budget to the legislature and appointing people to important positions within the executive and judicial branches.

The governor and his or her assistant, the lieutenant governor, are elected on a joint ballot. That means both the governor and the lieutenant governor are from the same political party. In the event that the governor dies or becomes too ill to serve his or her term, the lieutenant governor takes over the job. Other executive branch officers are the comptroller of the treasury, who oversees financial affairs, and the attorney general, the state's legal adviser.

Maryland's current governor, Martin O'Malley, was raised in the cities of Bethesda and Rockville. His family's heroes were people like Martin Luther King Jr. and John F. Kennedy. O'Malley's journey to high school took him past neighborhoods filled with homeless and unemployed people. He said, "That was not lost to many of us walking into school . . . every day, how lucky we were, how much we had."

A desire to help people inspired O'Malley to work on other people's campaigns before deciding to run for office himself. He served on the Baltimore City Council and was elected mayor of Baltimore twice. He was sworn in as governor on January 17, 2007.

After taking office, O'Malley began several initiatives designed to help Maryland's citizens. Previous increases in state spending, coupled with tax cuts, had left Maryland with a $1.4 billion budget deficit. O'Malley challenged the state's cabinet secretaries to cut their offices' spending by $200 million to set an example for other parts of the government. Then he asked each agency to cut spending by an average of 2.5 percent initially and then to cut as much as possible on top of that. "We need to . . . squeeze spending by working smarter," said the governor.

Governor Martin O'Malley speaks at Bowie State University as then–presidential hopeful Barack Obama looks on.

O'Malley's initial plan included reducing travel, cutting staff, consolidating offices, centralizing purchasing, and reducing staff overtime.

When it came time for concrete actions instead of plans, the governor led the way by making changes in his own office. He eliminated half of his office's vehicle fleet, and he encouraged other offices to cut the number of vehicles they use. Maryland's state departments own a total of approximately nine thousand cars, costing Maryland taxpayers $55 million to maintain in fiscal year 2007.

O'Malley also announced the formation of the Maryland Homeownership Preservation Task Force, which is charged with finding ways to prevent home foreclosures. (A foreclosure happens when a home owner becomes unable to continue to pay their home loan, and the home is sold by the bank.) June 2007 was declared Home Ownership Month. The governor said, "Homeownership in our state and in our country is the key to a stronger, growing middle class, and we must do all that we can to protect homeownership throughout Maryland."

Legislative Branch

The legislative branch creates and votes on Maryland's laws. It is made up of the Maryland General Assembly, which consists of a 141-member house of delegates and a 47-member senate. The term for all legislators is four years. Legislators in either house may introduce a bill. Once both houses have passed it and the governor has signed it, the bill becomes law.

The Maryland General Assembly begins meeting on the second Wednesday in January and stays in session for ninety days. During the legislative sessions from 2000 to 2005, an average of 907 bills per session were introduced. This means some of the bills do not have time to go through the entire process within ninety days. Legislators try to get their bills introduced as early in the session schedule as possible.

If a legislator gets his or her bill onto the schedule before the session even starts, it is introduced on the opening day.

Every year, the governor submits a budget to the general assembly. Legislators have the opportunity to reduce spending that the governor has proposed, but not to increase it. If the session is going to end within seven days and no budget bill has been passed, the governor has the power to extend the session. Once the budget has passed, the governor may not veto, or reject, it.

Despite the fact that Maryland was a slave state, Maryland's first constitution allowed both white and black males who met minimum property requirements to vote. A man had to own at least 50 acres in the county in which he wished to vote—or he had to have at least thirty pounds in "current money" and residence in the county for at least a year. Although the right to vote was later limited to white males for a time, Maryland's original spirit of inclusion has remained an important part of its culture and a source of state pride.

Judicial Branch

The judicial branch interprets laws and tries legal cases. Maryland's court system has four levels: the District Court of Maryland (the lowest court), the circuit courts, the Court of Special Appeals, and the Court of Appeals. The Court of Appeals, Maryland's highest court, consists of seven judges. These judges review important cases whose decisions must be based on interpretation of Maryland's constitution. In general, the governor appoints the four courts' judges. In some cases, including the Court of Appeals, voters must approve the appointed judges after their term has started.

In 1819, Maryland's courts were part of a landmark decision by the U.S. Supreme Court called *McCulloch v. Maryland*. Originally, the American colonies printed their own money and had their own banks, but a national banking system slowly emerged. In 1816, Congress established the Second National Bank to help prevent states from printing unregulated currency. Maryland reacted to this decision by passing a law that taxed banks not chartered by the state itself.

A cashier at the Baltimore branch of the Second National Bank, James W. McCulloch, refused to pay the state tax. Maryland sued him, and the case went before the U.S. Supreme Court. However, the Supreme Court concluded that establishing a nationwide banking system was within the power of Congress and that states did not have the power to tax institutions of the federal government.

In the court's decision, Chief Justice John Marshall wrote, "The Court has bestowed on this subject its most deliberate consideration. The result is a conviction that the States have no power, by taxation or otherwise, to retard, impede, burden, or in any manner control, the operations of the constitutional laws enacted by Congress. . . . This is a tax on the operations of the bank, and is, consequently, a tax on the operation of an instrument employed by the government of the Union to carry its powers into execution. Such a tax must be unconstitutional."

LOCAL GOVERNMENTS

Compared to many other states, Maryland has a low number of local governments because it has only twenty-three counties. Within these counties exist several types of local governments.

Eight counties (Calvert, Carroll, Cecil, Frederick, Garrett, St. Mary's, Somerset, and Washington) have county commissioners. The commissioners may enact ordinances (laws affecting their local community only), but their legislative power is limited by the Maryland General Assembly.

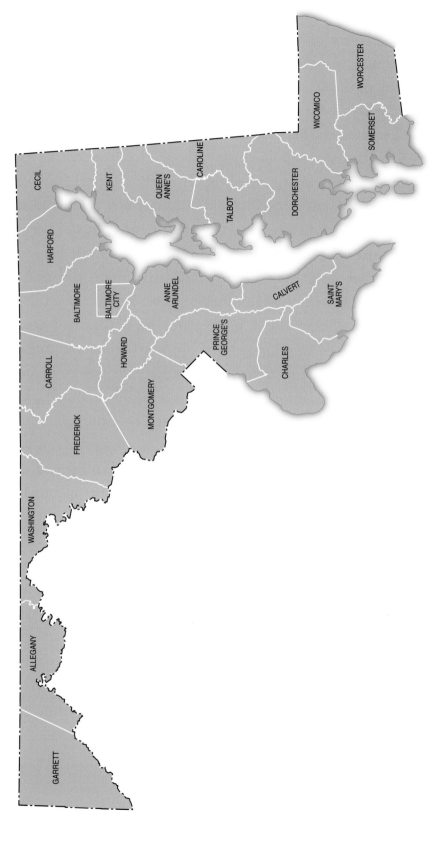

MARYLAND BY COUNTY

Other counties have something called code home rule. This allows them to exercise much broader authority over the legislation that is enacted in their counties. Without code home rule, issues such as noise restrictions, public safety, and the internal organization of local governments must be sent to Annapolis to be handled by the Maryland General Assembly. With code home rule, these issues can be handled at the local level. Six counties (Allegany, Caroline, Charles, Kent, Queen Anne's, Worcester) have chosen this form of government.

The rest of Maryland's counties operate under a charter government. This kind of local government separates the executive and legislative branches. It generally has both a county executive and a county council. Maryland's charter government counties are Anne Arundel, Baltimore, Dorchester, Harford, Howard, Montgomery, Prince George's, Talbot, and Wicomico.

CURRENT ISSUES

Today's Marylanders are divided on the issue of where to put their roads. State officials have proposed building a highway called the Inter-County Connector (ICC) to connect Interstate 95, which is northeast of Washington, D.C., with Gaithersburg, which lies northwest of the city. "We need to do everything to help solve the traffic congestion we are facing, [and] the ICC is the most important piece," said Montgomery County executive Douglas M. Duncan.

Marylanders have debated the highway for years. The Environmental Protection Agency favored the northern route but noted that building to the north would require the state to destroy about eighty more homes than it would with the projected southern route. As Maryland's roads get ever more congested and commuting times grow, the decision about where—or whether—to build becomes more critical.

BALTIMORE'S INNOVATIVE MAYOR

Kurt L. Schmoke became Baltimore's first elected African-American mayor on November 3, 1987. Schmoke was born in Baltimore and attended public schools before going on to Yale University in Connecticut and Oxford University in England, where he was a Rhodes Scholar. He then earned his law degree at Harvard. After working with President Jimmy Carter's domestic-policy staff, Schmoke returned to Baltimore. Eventually he was elected state's attorney, the city's chief prosecutor, an office he held until he became mayor.

During his three terms in office, Mayor Schmoke developed a reputation as one of the most innovative mayors in the nation. He tackled Baltimore's problems with energy and new ideas. Shortly after becoming mayor, he attacked the problem of illiteracy by declaring Baltimore The City That Reads. It was more than a catchy slogan. The mayor established a high-level city agency devoted to literacy and started a private foundation that funded and expanded literacy programs throughout the city.

As mayor, Schmoke was unafraid to try new approaches to old problems. He supported a policy that viewed drug abuse as a public-health problem, not just a law enforcement issue. He also suggested legalizing or decriminalizing drugs. This made him a controversial—yet always interesting—figure.

Federal approval for the $2.4 billion needed to build the ICC was given in 2006. In March 2007, Governor O'Malley said, "It is time to get to work. With the award of [the] first major construction contract, we are moving forward." The ICC is due to be completed in 2011 or 2012. However, opponents continue to argue that the new highway will not significantly reduce traffic and will destroy the local environment.

Another controversy involves the state's wildlife. In 2004, hundreds of Marylanders and others gathered in Annapolis to oppose the first black bear hunt in Maryland in over fifty years, which had been approved by then-governor Robert Ehrlich.

The black bear population of Maryland is just over three hundred. People who support the hunt claim that bears are a nuisance to people and a threat to livestock. They point to the fact that Maryland's bear population has rebounded since dropping to only twelve in the 1950s. People opposed to the hunt say that the particular bears killed during a hunting season might not be the ones that are bothering farmers and their animals. They also argue that Maryland's bear population is still threatened by loss of habitat, low reproductive rates, and hunting in other states.

Despite the protests, the 2004 season went off as planned. Hunters met the quota of twenty bears in one day. Another hunt was held in 2005. An eight-year-old girl became the first hunter to kill a bear in that season. Protests continue, but Maryland's yearly bear hunt is scheduled to continue into the foreseeable future.

Chapter Five

Going Global, Green, and High-Tech

Baltimore's location has always been a good one for transportation. With its central location between the northern and southern states, as well as its access to both rail and sea, Baltimoreans can move goods to and from other areas quickly. Today, much of Baltimore's economy is still tied up in the transportation of goods. Baltimore's port contributes over $1 billion per year to the state's economy. Baltimore/Washington International Thurgood Marshall Airport manages over 55,000 passengers per day. The airport employs more than ten thousand people in both full-time and part-time jobs and contributes an estimated $5.7 billion to Maryland's economy annually.

The cost of living in a big city like Baltimore is generally high. However, Baltimore is more affordable than some other large cities, such as Miami, New York City, or Washington, D.C. Everywhere in the United States, the costs of food, utilities, and housing rise steadily from year to year.

Maryland's economy relies on service industries. Here, a scientist uses a laser scan microscope to conduct research on diabetes.

Although Baltimore's home prices have increased considerably, Baltimoreans have not yet faced the same kinds of increases as people in other cities. Between 2000 and the first quarter of 2006, the average home cost in the Washington, D.C., area rose 170 percent to $422,500. Average house prices in Miami rose 175 percent to $377,000. By comparison, prices remained more stable in Baltimore. Average house prices rose 125 percent, to $265,900, in the same time period.

Still, the price of a home in Baltimore went up four times as much as the average Marylander's salary. This made buying a home more difficult for many people. To compensate, people are moving farther away from their jobs, which increases commuting times and clogs the highway systems even further. Rural and suburban schools are becoming more crowded, and land that was once used to grow food is now acre after acre of new homes. Some people would like to see more redevelopment near downtown Baltimore. This would get people closer to their jobs and would save the remaining wilderness and farmland. In 2006, the Maryland Association of Realtors planned to spend at least $1 million to educate people about programs that help make home ownership more affordable. Alan R. Ingraham, president of the association, said, "The focus is not just on entry-level homebuyers but on all segments of the housing market." The campaign will be called "We Bring You Home."

While Marylanders are concerned about housing costs, they also have much to celebrate. Maryland has one of the lowest child poverty rates in the United States. It is also home to some of the most educated towns in the United States. For example, over 44 percent of the population of the city of Potomac has at least one graduate degree. Bethesda and Chevy Chase have even higher percentages—47 percent and 48 percent respectively. All told, more than one-third of Marylanders have at least one college degree, and 13.7 percent have graduate or professional degrees. Maryland ranks number one among all fifty states in the education level of its citizens.

Maryland is the home of many great universities, including Johns Hopkins, which was founded in 1876. The university is well known for research yet particularly noted for its involvement of undergraduates. Nearly 80 percent of the undergraduates at Johns Hopkins are involved in some form of independent research alongside the top scientists in their fields.

In the first half of 2007, Maryland had one of the lowest rates of unemployment (3.9 percent) in the country. In 2004, the average income of the state's citizens was $39,247—19 percent higher than the national average of $32,937. These numbers paint a picture of overall economic health in the state of Maryland.

2006 GROSS STATE PRODUCT: $257.8 Billion

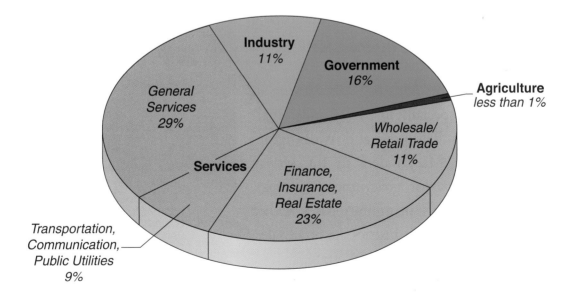

MAKING A LIVING

Maryland's economy—like the state itself—is very diverse. This is what you would expect from a state that contains the Chesapeake Bay, farmland, suburban Washington, D.C., and Baltimore—the country's eighteenth-largest city.

Maryland is a technology leader. The state is home to several key federal laboratories and agencies, including the National Institutes of Health, the Goddard Space Flight Center, and the Food and Drug Administration. High-tech companies that manufacture electronic components are attracted to Maryland because they know they will find well-educated, trained workers. Maryland also has more than three hundred bioscience firms, including Celera Genomics, Gene Logic, and Guilford Pharmaceuticals.

Although it has diminished over time, a strong manufacturing base is still important to Maryland. Companies such as General Motors, as well as other high-tech and defense manufacturing companies, maintain major facilities in the state.

The service industry is also strong in Maryland, especially in the 40-mile corridor between Baltimore and Washington, D.C. Many Marylanders in the service industry work for government agencies, schools, hospitals, or military bases. Other important service industries are retail sales, insurance, banking, and real estate.

At NASA's Goddard Space Flight Center, lab technicians test a component of the Hubble Space Telescope.

EARNING A LIVING

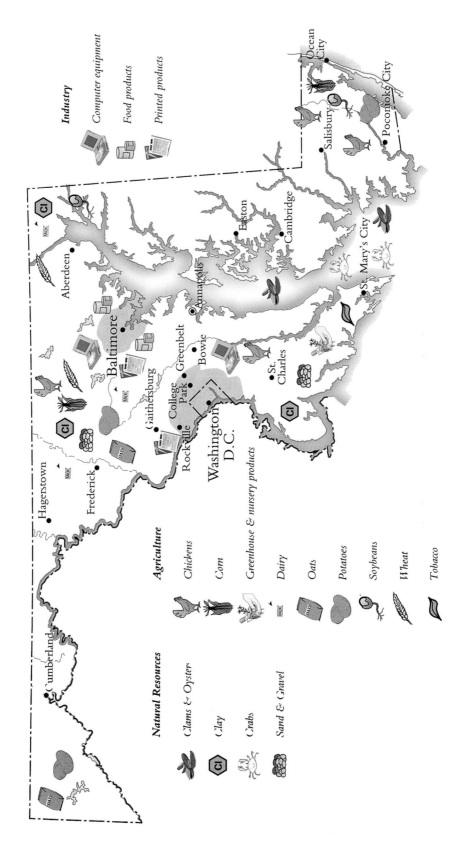

Industry
Computer equipment
Food products
Printed products

Agriculture
Chickens
Corn
Greenhouse & nursery products
Dairy
Oats
Potatoes
Soybeans
Wheat
Tobacco

Natural Resources
Clams & Oysters
Clay
Crabs
Sand & Gravel

Cumberland
Hagerstown
Frederick
Aberdeen
Baltimore
Gaithersburg
Rockville
College Park
Greenbelt
Bowie
Washington D.C.
Annapolis
St. Charles
St. Mary's City
Easton
Cambridge
Salisbury
Ocean City
Pocomoke City

Tourism also plays an important role in Maryland's economy. Thanks to its redeveloped Inner Harbor area, Baltimore now draws almost five million visitors every year. Ocean City, Maryland's largest resort town, attracts more than eight million visitors each summer—the town swells from 7,500 to as many as 300,000 people! Statewide, travel and tourism account for more than 86,000 jobs.

Western Maryland is a coal-producing region. The amount of coal mined today doesn't reach the historic highs of the early 1900s, however. Marble and limestone also are mined in western Maryland.

Tourism plays a major role in Baltimore's economy.

LINKING EAST AND WEST

As early as the 1920s, Maryland's leaders dreamed of connecting the Eastern Shore with the rest of the state by spanning the Chesapeake Bay with a bridge. However, the Great Depression, followed by World War II, delayed any action. In 1947, when the idea of a bridge came up again, there was nothing to stop it—except the many people who were opposed to it!

Ferryboat operators knew that a bridge would put them out of business. Shipping companies were afraid ships would run into the bridge during foggy weather. Some people on the Eastern Shore didn't want a bridge because they resisted outsiders and change. One group sang, "We don't give a darn for the whole state of Maryland; we're from the Eastern Shore!"

Business leaders on the Eastern Shore recognized that a bridge would lead to new markets for farm produce and would attract companies and new jobs. Ocean City pushed hard for a bridge because it would bring more tourists to the beaches. Finally, the bridge was approved. The two-lane Chesapeake Bay Bridge opened to the public in 1952, and a second span opened in 1973. After the new span was opened, the original bridge carried only eastbound traffic, while the new span carried westbound traffic.

Even now the bridge is breathtaking. Its spans gracefully rise 354 feet above the shimmering bay. Perhaps the best way to see the bridge and the bay in all their glory is on foot. One Sunday each May, a span of the bridge is closed to traffic, and thousands of Marylanders stroll 4.3 miles to the other side as part of the Chesapeake Bay Bridge Walk.

AN ECONOMY IN TRANSITION

Maryland has a vital role to play in a more globalized economy. Currently, nearly one in seven manufacturing workers in Maryland depends on exports for their jobs, and this number is expected to increase. Companies increasingly need employees who are comfortable working with people from other countries and speaking languages besides English.

The largest global player in the world's economy today is China. Trade with China has become an important part of Maryland's economy. In 2005, Maryland exported $284 million in goods to the Chinese market. That number is likely to grow over time. The state's schools have responded to the trend. Some Maryland high school students are being given the opportunity to learn Mandarin Chinese.

"Typically, Americans haven't been all that sensitive to local language and local customs," said Aris Melissaratos, secretary of the Maryland Department of Business and Economic Development. "We must learn the languages and we must learn the cultures if we want to compete." Training students in Mandarin will be a good start.

While many Europeans speak two or even three languages, fluency in multiple languages is less common in the United States. As the global economy grows, however, it becomes increasingly important for students to learn new languages in school. The state's future workers must build relationships among people and companies so that Maryland can compete internationally in the twenty-first century. "This will pay some real dividends down the road in business," said Deborah Kielty, president and executive director of the World Trade Center Institute in Baltimore. "Probably nothing says 'I care about you' more than addressing someone in their native language."

Maryland's current major trading partner is not China, however. It is Canada. In 2004, Maryland exported more goods to Canada than it did to

BIOPHARMACEUTICALS IN MARYLAND

Maryland is leading the way in the science of biopharmaceuticals. This science involves developing pharmaceuticals like drugs and vaccines from biological ingredients such as insulin, proteins, or growth hormones. The first company to begin marketing biopharmaceuticals was Indianapolis-based Eli Lilly and Company, which began selling Humulin (a kind of insulin created in a lab) in 1982. Since then, many companies have developed therapies through biotechnology.

Many biopharmaceutical companies are based in Maryland. One is Human Genome Sciences, whose headquarters are in Rockville. This company's inventions include Albuferon® and ABthrax™. Albuferon® is currently undergoing clinical trials, but if it proves successful and is approved by the Food and Drug Administration, it will be used to treat diseases such as hepatitis C, which is one of the most common chronic blood-borne infections in the United States. An estimated four million Americans suffer from hepatitis C; worldwide, 170 million people have the disease. Albuferon® could help decrease the side effects of treatment for hepatitis C.

Human Genome Sciences plans to use ABthrax™ to treat anthrax. Anthrax is an often-fatal bacterial disease that can survive for years, even decades, in a powdered form. In 2001, criminals used anthrax as a weapon by sending powder-laced letters through the mail. Five people died of the disease. Human Genome Sciences hopes that its drug will prove useful in saving lives with minimal side effects.

China, Japan, and Great Britain combined. The leading exports were unshaped plastics, books, trucks, automobiles, pigments, and toners. Maryland's main imports from Canada are softwood lumber, newsprint, iron ore, and electrical lighting equipment.

In 2004, exports to Canada totaled $896 million. The state imported $1.6 billion in goods from Canada. Besides goods, tourists also traveled between the two areas. About 189,000 Canadians visited Maryland and spent $32 million in the state. During the same time period, 213,500 Marylanders traveled to Canada and spent $119 million.

Maryland's economy also benefits from Canadian companies such as Marada Industries Inc., Canam Steel Corporation, and BCE Emergis Corporation. The Maryland-based offices and plants of these companies support more than 100,000 jobs.

SMALL BUSINESS

Small businesses also fuel Maryland's economy. The federal government defines a small business as "one that is independently owned and operated and which is not dominant in its field of operation." There are about 443,000 small businesses in Maryland. Of these, 29 percent (128,000) are owned by women, and 25 percent (115,000) are minority-owned. Small businesses are an important source of taxes and employment. At least 47 percent of Marylanders who work full-time or part-time have jobs in small businesses.

Nearly 65 percent of Maryland's small businesses are microenterprises, meaning they have five or fewer employees. Such businesses include tailors, car repair shops, dry cleaners, daycare providers, caterers, arts and crafts stores, and fishing-boat charter companies. These businesses face unique obstacles. The founder of a microbusiness might know

A small business in Baltimore

very little about running a business. In addition, tiny companies have a difficult time getting help from government or local agencies.

Business owners can turn to the Microenterprise Council of Maryland (MCM). This organization offers business development services such as training, helping with marketing campaigns, and helping businesses secure affordable loans and government certification. MCM trains people to use the Internet to help their business and to network within the community. The organization also brings together business owners who are facing the same obstacles.

MARYLAND WORKFORCE

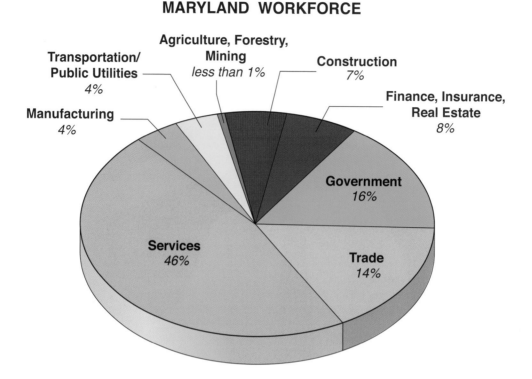

Transportation/Public Utilities 4%

Agriculture, Forestry, Mining *less than 1%*

Construction 7%

Manufacturing 4%

Finance, Insurance, Real Estate *8%*

Government *16%*

Services *46%*

Trade *14%*

GETTING GREEN

As energy costs rise, Marylanders have begun to look for alternatives to traditional energy sources. One approach is to build "green" homes and businesses. Green homes have solar panels to collect energy from the sun, as well as other energy-saving devices. Maryland has implemented the Green Building Tax Credit, which gives businesses and nonprofit organizations a tax break when they construct buildings that meet state environmental guidelines. Individuals are encouraged to use recycled or local materials when building or to use sustainable materials such as bamboo.

Homes equipped with solar panels and other energy-saving devices save people money. They can even produce enough electricity to make the electric meter on the house go backward! That means the house is giving energy to the power company, and the home owner gets a discount on his or her bill.

The current downside to green technology is that it often costs more to retrofit a home with solar panels than a home owner could make back in utility savings. As the costs of heating and cooling a house continue to rise, however, strategies like solar panels may become more cost-effective in older homes.

Another way to save energy is to heat and cool a building using geothermal power—energy that comes from the earth. In Carroll County, the Finksburg branch of the public library system is one of the first buildings in Maryland to use geothermal power. The system is initially more expensive to put in than traditional heating and cooling systems, but savings are so great that the system will pay for itself within six years. If energy prices continue to rise, it could pay for itself much earlier than that.

The library depends on sixty wells, each 400 feet deep. The wells pump geothermal energy into the building. In winter, the soil of the earth is warmer than the air, so the building is warm. In summer, the soil is cooler than the air, so the building stays cool.

Other Maryland buildings using the geothermal system include schools in Montgomery and Dorchester counties, as well as Ebb Valley Elementary School in Carroll.

Chapter Six
Maryland's Treasures

Maryland is a small state, but that doesn't mean there is little to see or to do. On the contrary, Maryland is chock-full of exciting places to visit, ranging from the mountains to the ocean, the city to the country, the glamorous to the simple, and the old to the new. The Old Line State holds many treasures for both locals and visitors.

SWITZERLAND OF AMERICA

With its mountains, twisting trails, and waterfalls, western Maryland still has a feeling of wildness about it. In the mid-1800s, this part of Maryland was known as the Switzerland of America because of its picturesque mountains.

People take advantage of western Maryland's beautiful landscape to pursue outdoor activities. The state's largest lake, the man-made Deep Creek Lake, is great for boating, swimming, and fishing. Some people even scuba dive as they search for relics in farmhouses that were submerged when the lake was created in the 1920s. Thousands of homes and cottages line the shore. "It's a great place to go in the summer when you want to beat the heat," said Marylander Cecilia Sager.

At Ego Alley in Annapolis, boat owners parade their prized possessions.

PLACES TO SEE

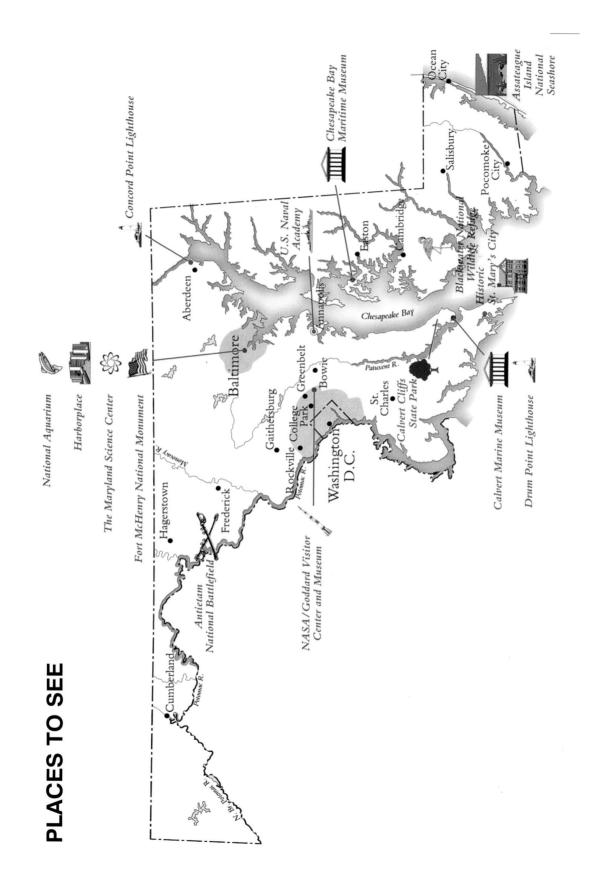

National Aquarium

Harborplace

The Maryland Science Center

Fort McHenry National Monument

Concord Point Lighthouse

Chesapeake Bay Maritime Museum

U.S. Naval Academy

Baltimore

Aberdeen

Chesapeake Bay

Easton

Cambridge

Salisbury

Blackwater National Wildlife Refuge

Historic St. Mary's City

Pocomoke City

Ocean City

Assateague Island National Seashore

Gaithersburg

Rockville

College Park

Greenbelt

Bowie

Patuxent R.

St. Charles

Calvert Cliffs State Park

Washington D.C.

Potomac R.

Monocacy R.

Frederick

Hagerstown

Antietam National Battlefield

NASA/Goddard Visitor Center and Museum

Cumberland

Potomac R.

N. Br. Potomac R.

Calvert Marine Museum

Drum Point Lighthouse

Wherever you are in Maryland, you're never more than a few minutes away from a state park or forest. The state owns more than 280,000 acres of forests, fields, marshes, lakes, rivers, and beaches. The first state forest was set aside in 1906 at Swallow Falls, a beautiful cascade of water that attracts hikers.

Where there are mountains, there is skiing! Wisp Resort offers downhill skiing from December to mid-March. There are also ample state parks where people can enjoy cross-country skiing.

Antietam National Battlefield, near Sharpsburg, is the site of the bloodiest battle of the Civil War. On September 17, 1862, more than 23,000 soldiers were killed there as Confederate forces tried to drive the war northward. Union general Joseph Hooker wrote of the battle, "The slain lay in rows precisely as they had stood in their ranks a few moments before." Today, the peaceful, green park has replaced the scene of destruction.

Civil War cannons rest on the battlefield at Antietam.

Visitors to the battlefield can trace the phases of the battle by stopping at such spots as Burnside Bridge, where a few Georgia riflemen held off Union soldiers for most of the day, and Bloody Lane, the site of a four-hour battle that resulted in four thousand deaths. A visit to the cemetery is a sobering experience. The visitor's center features an audiovisual presentation that provides background and perspective on the battle.

Near the battlefield is Fort Frederick, the only surviving stone fortification from the French and Indian War (1754–1763). The fort was built in 1756.

CENTRAL MARYLAND

Visitors to Central Maryland will be surprised at the variety of attractions. Much of the area is farmland, with rolling hills of horse farms, quiet towns, and back roads where you can still find covered bridges. This region is also home to the thriving city of Baltimore and the state capital of Annapolis.

Baltimore: Charm City

Baltimore, Maryland's biggest city, has reinvented itself as a tourist destination during the past twenty-five years. The downtown waterfront has been rebuilt into a series of shops, restaurants, and museums called Harborplace. The National Aquarium features dolphin shows, shark feedings, and educational displays about marine life. From the observation deck on the twenty-seventh floor of the World Trade Center, you can look out over the city and beyond to the Chesapeake Bay. Another Harborplace highlight is the U.S. frigate *Constellation*. Built in 1797, this ship was used during the War of 1812, the Civil War, and World War II before being retired.

From Harborplace, tourists can take a water taxi to destinations throughout the city. The funky neighborhood of Fells Point features

Dolphins perform at a show at the National Aquarium in Baltimore.

historic houses, shops, restaurants, and the Broadway Market, which is known for its Polish food stands and butcher shops. The Baltimore Museum of Industry traces the city's roots as a port city and industrial leader. The Maryland Science Center has live science demonstrations and three floors of hands-on exhibits. The childhood home of Babe Ruth, one of baseball's greatest players, has been restored. Exhibits there include rare photos, baseball memorabilia, and game highlights.

The B&O Railroad Museum exhibits more than 120 pieces of full-size equipment, including steam, diesel, and electric locomotives and a large collection of railroad artifacts. Fort McHenry houses exhibits about the War of 1812, when a flag flying high above the fort inspired Francis Scott Key to write "The Star-Spangled Banner."

"There's so much more to Baltimore than you'd expect," said resident Kristy Doty. "No wonder they call it Charm City!"

The B&O Railroad Museum in Baltimore displays more than 120 full-size locomotives.

AND THEY'RE OFF!

Baltimore's Pimlico Race Course is the site of one of the most important horse races in the United States: the Preakness Stakes, held each May. This race is part of the Triple Crown, along with the Kentucky Derby and the Belmont Stakes. A horse that wins all three races receives the high honor of Triple Crown winner.

The Preakness started in 1873, two years before the Kentucky Derby. The first race drew seven starters and about 12,000 spectators. Now nearly 100,000 people go to watch the horses run the race, which covers 1³/₁₆ miles.

After the winner has been declared, a painter climbs a ladder to the top of a replica of the Old Clubhouse cupola in the winner's circle. There is a weathervane in the shape of a horse and jockey on the cupola. The artist paints the colors of the new winner's silks on the jockey and horse as everyone cheers.

One official painter said, "It is just the thrill of being able to participate in a big local and national event like this. Let's face it, it's the only televised . . . painting job in the country."

Annapolis

The state house in Annapolis is the oldest continuously operating state capitol in the country. Annapolis, chartered in 1708, is one of the country's oldest cities. Tourists flock there to stroll along the city's picturesque brick streets and to stop at antique shops, restored historic houses, restaurants, and boutiques. No walk through Annapolis is complete without pausing for a few moments at the waterfront to watch the parade of boats pass through. "We call it Ego Alley because there's a lot of showing off," said one Annapolis resident.

Midshipmen graduate at the U.S. Naval Academy in Annapolis.

TEN LARGEST CITIES

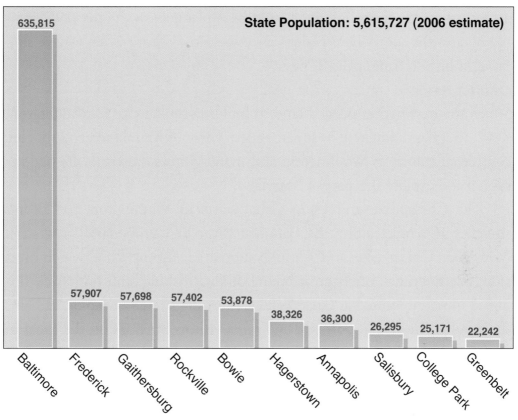

State Population: 5,615,727 (2006 estimate)

City	Population
Baltimore	635,815
Frederick	57,907
Gaithersburg	57,698
Rockville	57,402
Bowie	53,878
Hagerstown	38,326
Annapolis	36,300
Salisbury	26,295
College Park	25,171
Greenbelt	22,242

Annapolis is also home to the U.S. Naval Academy, established in 1845. While touring its buildings and grounds, you may catch sight of a traditional wedding at the chapel, where midshipmen create an arch of sabers for the newly married couple to pass under. Naval Academy graduate Major John Scanlan of the U.S. Marine Corps said, "The last guy in the line taps the bride with his saber and says, 'Welcome to the navy!'"

While Annapolis hosts many festivals, one of the most popular is the Kunta Kinte Heritage Festival. This celebration honors the enslaved African man whose story Alex Haley told in his best-selling book *Roots*.

The festival includes storytelling, costumed African dancers, and special activities for kids, including mask making. A plaque near the city dock commemorates the spot where Haley's ancestor came ashore when a slave ship brought him to America in 1767.

Capital Region

When the new nation needed land to build its capital city of Washington, D.C., Maryland donated 70 square miles. Three of Maryland's counties are considered suburban Washington, and many visitors drawn to the nation's capital also explore this part of Maryland.

The Chesapeake and Ohio Canal starts in Washington, D.C., and stretches 184 miles along the Potomac River to Cumberland in western Maryland. Chesapeake and Ohio National Historical Park, which runs alongside the canal, offers great biking, hiking, fishing, and horseback riding. A museum located at Great Falls, a churning stretch of rapids, explains the canal's historical importance and takes visitors for rides on the canal in an authentic mule-driven boat.

SOUTHERN MARYLAND

In southern Maryland you can visit the site of the state's first permanent European settlement, St. Mary's City. It is now a living museum, where costumed interpreters tell visitors about life in the seventeenth century. The 800-acre complex includes the Godiah Spray Tobacco Plantation, a working reconstruction of a seventeenth-century tobacco plantation, and the *Maryland Dove*, a replica of one of the ships that brought the original settlers from England.

If St. Mary's City isn't old enough for you, check out Calvert Cliffs State Park and Flag Ponds Nature Park. Visitors hunt for the fossilized remains of giant sharks and other sea creatures that roamed the waters fifteen million

A woman in colonial dress tends to a pot in historic St. Mary's City.

years ago. The parks have trails, wetlands boardwalks, and visitors' centers with displays about the local wildlife.

Solomons Island is now connected to the mainland by a bridge built on a bed of oyster shells, but it still has the feel of the isolated fishing village it once was. The town's main attraction is the Calvert Marine Museum, which features displays about boatbuilding, plant and animal life of the Chesapeake Bay, and fossils from Calvert Cliffs.

EASTERN SHORE

Maryland's Eastern Shore is framed by the Chesapeake Bay to the west and the Atlantic Ocean and Delaware to the east. Hardly a forgotten corner of the state, this region is now a popular tourist destination.

KING OYSTER'S FESTIVAL

St. Mary's County has an unusual claim to fame. It's the site of the National Oyster Shucking Championship, held every October as part of the St. Mary's Oyster Festival. Men and women who make their living shucking, or shelling, oysters vie for the title of U.S. National Oyster Shucking Champion. The winner gets a free trip to the world championship held in Ireland.

The champion is judged on speed and skill. The oyster must be cut completely apart from the shell with the sharp knife with as few broken bits of shell mixed in as possible. Members of the audience cheer their favorite shucker and eagerly await the end of each round, when the shuckers pass their opened oysters to the crowd. "They don't get much fresher than this," said one Marylander with a mouthful.

If raw oysters aren't your favorite food, there are plenty of cooked ones—fried, scalded, and cooked in stew. The luckiest people are the judges of the National Oyster Cook-Off, which draws more than four hundred entries from all over the country. Through it all, the festival's mascot, King Oyster, roams through the crowds and makes sure everyone is having fun and getting enough to eat.

Families from throughout the East Coast travel to Ocean City during the summer months. "You feel like you've entered another world once you're over," commented Mike Hansen, who spends many summer weekends there. The town features beaches, water sports, fishing, and a fun-filled boardwalk.

Many watermen earn extra money by taking visitors out on the bay in their boats. They share stories and tall tales, demonstrate how to dredge for oysters, and offer a brief taste of life on the water.

When you want to learn to the difference between a skipjack and a bugeye, there's no better place to go than the Chesapeake Bay Maritime Museum in St. Michaels. This picturesque Eastern Shore town was a shipbuilding center in the late eighteenth and early nineteenth centuries. The museum exhibits bay craft, guns and decoys, and ship models. (A bugeye was a boat watermen used for dredging oysters before skipjacks were developed in the 1890s. It was bigger and didn't have the distinctive V-shaped bottom of a skipjack.)

Duck hunting is an important part of Maryland's heritage, and the carving of duck decoys has evolved into an art form. The decoys at the Ward Museum of Wildfowl Art in Salisbury are so beautiful (and expensive) that no collector would dare put them in the water.

To see the real thing, head to the Blackwater National Wildlife Refuge near Cambridge, where migratory waterfowl such as ducks, geese, and swans rest and feed from mid-October to December. The refuge is also home to bald eagles and endangered Delmarva fox squirrels.

All of this is just a glimpse of what Maryland offers. There's so much more to see and do! Maryland is truly an exciting state to visit.

THE FLAG: The red and white quarters of the flag are the coat of arms of the Crosslands. The black and gold quarters are that of the Calverts.

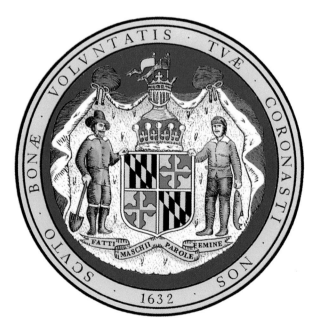

THE SEAL: The front of the state seal shows Lord Baltimore dressed in armor riding a horse along the seashore. On the back a farmer and a fisherman are standing next to a shield bearing the coats of arms of the Calverts and the Crosslands, two branches of Lord Baltimore's family.

State Survey

Statehood: April 28, 1788

Origin of Name: named in honor of Queen Henrietta Maria, the wife of King Charles I of England

Nickname: Old Line State

Capital: Annapolis

Motto: Manly Deeds, Womanly Words *(Fatti maschii, parole feminine)*

Bird: Baltimore oriole *(Icterus galbula)*

Flower: black-eyed Susan *(Rudbeckia hirta)*

Tree: white oak *(Quercus alba)*

Insect: Baltimore checkerspot butterfly *(Euphydryas phaeion)*

Crustacean: Maryland blue crab *(Callinectes sapidus)*

Dog: Chesapeake Bay retriever

Fish: striped bass *(Morone saxatilis)*

Baltimore oriole

Black-eyed Susans

MARYLAND, MY MARYLAND

James R. Randall, who wrote the lyrics to this song in 1861, hoped his poem would inspire Maryland to join the Confederacy. Despite the song's great popularity, due in part to its well-known tune, Maryland did not secede from the Union. However, 138 years later—in 1939—"Maryland, My Maryland" was adopted as the official state song.

Words by James R. Randall   **Music: "Oh, Tannenbaum"**

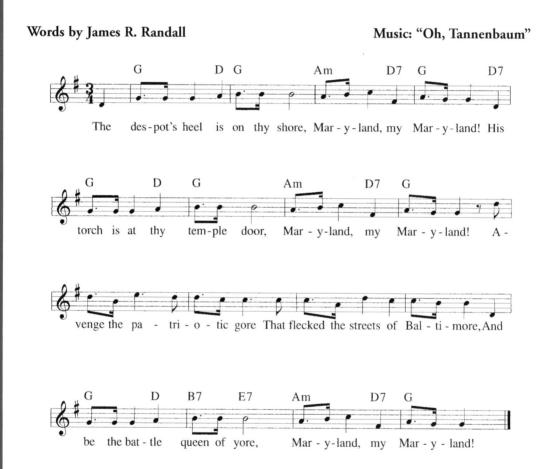

Folk dance: square dancing

Fossil shell: *Ecphora quadricostata*

Sport: jousting

Boat: skipjack

Dinosaur: *Astrodon johnstoni*

Drink: milk

GEOGRAPHY

Highest Point: 3,360 feet above sea level, at Blackbone Mountain

Lowest Point: sea level, along the Atlantic coast

Area: 10,455 square miles

Greatest Distance North to South: 124 miles

Greatest Distance East to West: 238 miles

Bordering States: Pennsylvania to the north, West Virginia to the west, Virginia to the south, Delaware to the east

Hottest Recorded Temperature: 109 °F at Cumberland and Frederick on July 10, 1936

Coldest Recorded Temperature: -40 °F at Oakland on January 13, 1912

Average Annual Precipitation: 43 inches

Major Rivers: Chester, Gunpowder, Nanticoke, Patapsco, Patuxent, Potomac, Susquehanna, Youghiogheny

Major Lakes: Deep Creek, Liberty, Loch Raven, Prettyboy

Trees: ash, beech, cypress, hemlock, hickory, maple, oak, red gum, spruce, tupelo, white pine

Wild Plants: azalea, black-eyed Susan, blackberry, dewberry, laurel, raspberry, rhododendron

Animals: chipmunk, cottontail rabbit, gray fox, mink, muskrat, opossum, otter, raccoon, red fox, squirrel, white-tailed deer, woodchuck

Birds: bluebird, cardinal, dove, duck, goose, great blue heron, grouse, mockingbird, partridge, plover, sandpiper, sparrow, starling, wild turkey, woodcock

Fish: bluefish, carp, croaker, sea trout, striped bass

Shellfish: crab, oyster, shrimp

Endangered Animals: American peregrine falcon, bog turtle, Delmarva fox squirrel, dwarf wedge mussel, Indiana bat, Maryland darter, northeastern beach tiger beetle, piping plover, Puritan tiger beetle

Endangered Plants: Canby's dropwort, harperella, northeastern bulrush, sandplain gerardia, sensitive joint-vetch, swamp pink

The endangered Delmarva fox squirrel

TIMELINE

Maryland History

c. 10,000 B.C.E. The first humans arrive in the area of present-day Maryland.

c. 1,500 B.C.E. Oysters become an important food source.

c. 1,000 B.C.E. Native Americans begin using pottery.

c. 800 C.E. Native people first use the bow and arrow.

1500s The Choptank, Nanticoke, Patuxent, Piscataway, Pocomoke, Portobago, Wicomico, and Susquehannock tribes live in the region.

1572 Spaniard Pedro Menéndez de Avilés becomes one of the first Europeans to enter the Chesapeake Bay.

1608 John Smith explores the Chesapeake Bay.

1631 William Claiborne establishes a trading post, the first European settlement in Maryland, on Kent Island.

1632 King Charles I of England grants Lord Baltimore the charter for the colony of Maryland.

1649 Maryland passes a religious toleration act.

1694 Maryland's capital moves from St. Mary's to Annapolis.

1727 The *Maryland Gazette*, the first newspaper in Maryland, is published weekly starting in September.

1729 Baltimore is founded.

1767 Charles Mason and Jeremiah Dixon complete their survey of the Maryland-Pennsylvania border and establish the Mason-Dixon Line.

1775 The American Revolution begins.

1776 Maryland establishes a state government as a result of independence.

1784 The Treaty of Paris, ending the American Revolution, is ratified in Annapolis.

1788 Maryland becomes the seventh state in the Union.

1791 Maryland contributes land for the District of Columbia.

1814 Francis Scott Key writes "The Star-Spangled Banner."

1828 Construction begins on the Baltimore and Ohio (B&O) Railroad.

1830 The *Tom Thumb*, the first American steam engine, begins operating between Baltimore and Ellicott's Mills.

1844 The first telegraph line in the United States begins operation between Baltimore and Washington, D.C.

1845 The U.S. Naval Academy is founded at Annapolis.

1861 The Civil War begins; Maryland remains in the Union.

1862 The Battle of Antietam is fought in western Maryland.

1864 Maryland abolishes slavery.

1867 Maryland adopts its fourth and present constitution.

1876 Johns Hopkins University opens in Baltimore.

1904 A fire destroys downtown Baltimore; Maryland adopts its state flag.

1937 The state legislature approves Maryland's first state income tax.

1952 The Chesapeake Bay Bridge (later renamed the William P. Lane Jr. Memorial Bridge), connecting the Eastern and Western shores, opens.

1954 Baltimore's public schools are desegregated.

1967 Marylander Thurgood Marshall becomes the first African-American justice on the U.S. Supreme Court.

1983 Maryland and neighboring states begin working to clean up the Chesapeake Bay.

1987 Kurt Lidell Schmoke becomes the first elected African-American mayor of Baltimore.

1988 Maryland celebrates its two hundredth birthday as a state.

1991 Vera Hall becomes the first African-American woman chair of the Maryland Democratic Party.

1992 Oriole Park at Camden Yards officially opens.

1995 Annapolis celebrates its three hundredth anniversary as the capital of Maryland.

1998 The state dedicates a memorial to the Marylanders who served in World War II across the Severn River from the Naval Academy in Annapolis. It is engraved with the names of the 6,454 Marylanders who died in the conflict; a Middle East peace summit is held at the Aspen Institute's Wye River Conference Centers in Queen Anne's County.

2000 The Maryland state quarter is released. It showcases the dome of the Maryland Statehouse, the year 1788, the motto "The Old Line State," and white oak leaves.

2001 The Baltimore Ravens win the Super Bowl.

2002 Electronic voting machines are first used in Maryland during primary elections in four counties (Allegany, Dorchester, Montgomery, and Prince George's).

2004 Maryland celebrates its Flag Centennial; an electronic voting system is used statewide during primary elections.

2006 The Chesapeake Bay Trust announces that it has distributed twenty million dollars in grants for projects to restore the bay since 1985.

2007 Maryland enacts the nation's first living wage law.

ECONOMY

Agricultural Products: cattle, chickens, corn, greenhouse and nursery plants, milk, soybeans, wheat

Manufactured Products: chemicals, electrical equipment, food products, printed materials, steel

Natural Resources: clay, crushed stone, fish, gravel, limestone, sand

Business and Trade: finance, health care, insurance, wholesale and retail trade

CALENDAR OF CELEBRATIONS

National Outdoor Show Log-sawing, duck-calling, and trap-setting contests make for a fun February weekend in Golden Hill.

Maple Syrup Demonstration and Mountain Heritage Festival Come watch the sap flow in Thurmont. At this March event, you can see tree-tapping and sap-boiling demonstrations and enjoy storytelling and old-fashioned carriage rides.

Celtic Festival of Southern Maryland Each April, people in St. Leonard kick up their heels at this celebration of all things Celtic. There's plenty of piping, fiddling, dancing, athletic competitions, food, and crafts from Scotland, Ireland, and Wales.

Maryland Preakness Celebration In Baltimore, the Preakness is more than just a horse race. It's also the end of a weeklong May celebration that features hot-air balloon races, parades, and concerts.

Chesapeake and Ohio Canal Festival Each May, Cumberland commemorates the importance of the canal with a festival that includes rides on a replica of a canal boat, horse-and-buggy rides, an ox roast, and a street dance.

Montgomery County International Festival At this June event, Silver Spring celebrates the more than eighty different cultures of the people who have settled there. You can sample foods ranging from Thai to Colombian to Australian and play games from around the world. International dancers, musicians, and crafts exhibits are also part of the festivities.

Strawberry Festival You'll want to be hungry for this festival honoring the June strawberry harvest in Thurmont. You can enjoy strawberry pies, shakes, shortcake, sundaes, drinks, and more. A strawberry-eating contest, folk music, and crafts displays add to the fun.

Ice Cream Festival Nearly 10,000 pounds of ice cream are eaten during this three-day July festival in Baltimore. You can eat yours in cones, floats, or sundaes. You can also taste new flavors that ice-cream makers are testing.

Friendsville Fiddle and Banjo Contest Every July since 1964, musicians from the Friendsville area have gotten together for a day filled with toe-tapping bluegrass and old-time country music.

Rocky Gap Country Music Bluegrass Festival Some of the brightest stars in country music gather in Cumberland each August for a busy weekend of concerts, workshops, sing-alongs, craft demonstrations, and various activities for children.

Old St. Joseph's Jousting Tournament and Horse Show Competitors test their skill at Maryland's official state sport at this August event in Easton. Besides watching horsemen try to spear rings, you can attend a horse show or a medieval pageant and enjoy lots of great food at a country picnic.

National Hard Crab Derby Crisfield calls itself the Crab Capital of America. Each September the town stakes its claim to this title by holding the largest seafood festival on the Chesapeake Bay. Events include a crab race, a crab-picking contest, the crowning of Miss Crustacean, and a fireworks display.

Polkamotion-by-the-Ocean Thousands of couples twirl the nights away to the sounds of the nation's best polka bands during this four-day September event in Ocean City.

St. Mary's County Oyster Festival The National Oyster Shucking Championship and the National Oyster Cook-Off are the big draws at this October extravaganza in Leonardtown. After you've had your fill of oysters prepared every possible way, you can shop at a flea market, watch a puppet show, or enjoy a hayride.

German Fest The emphasis at this October event in Thurmont is food. You can try German potato salad, bratwurst, dumplings, and strudel while listening to German accordion tunes.

Waterfowl Festival Displays of duck decoys, decoy-carving demonstrations, and duck- and goose-calling contests are all part of the fun when Easton celebrates the return of thousands of waterfowl for the winter each November.

Christmas in Annapolis Annapolis is at its loveliest and most festive during the Christmas season. During December, you can tour exquisitely decorated eighteenth-century homes, watch a parade of yachts festooned with lights, and join in candlelit caroling.

Christmas in Annapolis

Hon Fest Held in early June, this unique celebration celebrates the language and culture of the people of Baltimore. Come for the food, the street vendors, and the quirky shops. Watch women compete for the title of Best Hon with their beehive hairdos, blue eye shadow, and leopard print pants.

STATE STARS

Benjamin Banneker (1731–1806), an astronomer, mathematician, and surveyor, was one of the first recognized African-American scientists. The son of a free mother and a slave who had bought his own freedom, Banneker attended school for several years and then continued to read extensively. In the process, he taught himself astronomy. During Banneker's varied career, he helped to survey and to lay out Washington, D.C. He also published his own almanac containing astronomical, weather, and tide predictions. Banneker was born in Ellicott's Mills.

Eubie Blake (1883–1983), one of the nation's most gifted ragtime musicians and composers, was born in Baltimore. Blake grew up listening to ragtime's intricate, lively rhythms and began performing professionally as a teenager. He wrote his first important song, "The Charleston Rag," in 1899. Another of his well-known songs is "I'm Just Wild About Harry." In 1979, Blake's life and music were celebrated in a hit Broadway show called *Eubie*.

John Wilkes Booth (1837–1865) was the assassin of President Abraham Lincoln. Booth was a well-regarded actor whose sympathies lay with the South during the Civil War. He shot Lincoln at Ford's Theatre in Washington, D.C., and escaped to Maryland. He was tracked to Virginia, where he was found hiding in a tobacco barn owned by Richard H. Garrett. Booth refused to surrender and was shot to death by Sergeant Boston Corbett. Booth was born in Bel Air.

James M. Cain (1892–1977) was a master of tough, unsentimental crime fiction. Born in Annapolis, Cain began his career as a journalist in Baltimore and New York City. He eventually turned his attention to fiction. His first novel, *The Postman Always Rings Twice*, brought him fame. Many of Cain's novels, such as *Double Indemnity*, are classics of modern fiction.

Rachel Carson (1907–1964) was a marine biologist and environmental writer. Carson, who lived in Silver Spring, spent most of her career working for the U.S. Fish and Wildlife Service. She first earned fame for *The Sea Around Us*, which won the National Book Award and sat atop the best-seller list for thirty-nine weeks. She is best remembered, however, for her 1962 book *Silent Spring*, which warned Americans about the dangers of pesticides.

Tom Clancy (1947–   ) is the author of best-selling thrillers. Many of his books, including *The Hunt for Red October* and *Patriot Games*, have been made into popular motion pictures. Clancy was born in Baltimore. He now lives in Calvert County.

Frederick Douglass (1817–1895) was a writer and antislavery activist. Douglass was born a slave in Tuckahoe. He escaped to freedom in 1838 and quickly became a powerful voice in the antislavery movement. During the Civil War, Douglass lobbied President Abraham Lincoln to include African-American soldiers among Union forces, and he later tried to improve the troops' treatment. After the war, Douglass continued to speak out for civil rights and women's rights. He also held various government posts, including minister to Haiti.

Philip Glass (1937–) is an influential composer renowned for his trance-like music. Born in Baltimore, Glass was a gifted child. He entered the University of Chicago at age fourteen and later studied at New York's Juilliard School of Music. In the 1960s, he traveled to India and Tibet and discovered musical influences there. He began incorporating the rhythms of Eastern music into his work by creating repetitive compositions featuring layers of sound. His most famous work is the opera *Einstein on the Beach*.

Dashiell Hammett (1894–1961), a native of St. Mary's County, created a new type of detective fiction. Previously, mysteries had always featured glamorous detectives, but Hammett's characters were sloppy men doing an unglamorous job. Later, he created the unforgettable Sam Spade, the original wisecracking tough-guy detective. Hammett's classic novels include *The Maltese Falcon*, *Red Harvest*, and *The Thin Man*.

Matthew Henson (1866–1955), an African-American explorer from Charles County, was one of the first two men to reach the North Pole. Henson always had a love of adventure. At thirteen, he took a job on a ship bound for China. In 1888, he first worked for explorer Robert Peary. Three years later, they went to Greenland. Henson befriended Inuit, the native people who lived there, and learned their language. Peary and Henson returned to Greenland time and again in their attempt to reach the North Pole. According to most accounts, they finally succeeded in 1909.

Matthew Henson

Billie Holiday (1915–1959) was one of the greatest American jazz singers. From the time she first started singing at jazz clubs in Harlem, New York, Holiday stunned audiences. Her unusual phrasing made her songs sad, sensual, and poignant. In 1938, Holiday began singing with Artie Shaw, thus becoming one of the first African Americans to sing with a white orchestra. In 1972, her autobiography, *Lady Sings the Blues*, was made into a successful film. Holiday was born in Baltimore.

Billie Holiday

Johns Hopkins (1795–1873), a merchant, banker, and philanthropist from Anne Arundel County, gave his name to Maryland's most famous university and hospital. Hopkins became wealthy through his wholesale grocery business in Baltimore. He also helped organize the Baltimore and Ohio Railroad. When he died, he left millions of dollars to found Johns Hopkins University and Johns Hopkins Hospital.

Francis Scott Key (1779–1843), who was born in Frederick County, earned his place in history by writing "The Star-Spangled Banner." Key watched the British bombardment of Fort McHenry during the War of 1812. The following morning, when he saw the American flag still flying over the fort, he wrote the words to his famous poem. The poem was soon reprinted in newspapers throughout America, but it did not become the official national anthem of the United States until 1931.

Barry Levinson (1942–   ), a noted movie director and writer, is from Baltimore. His first film, *Diner*, is an affectionate look at growing up in 1950s Baltimore. Later films, such as *Tin Men* and *Avalon*, are also set in Baltimore. In 1988, Levinson's film *Rain Man*, a story about a brash young man and his autistic brother, won several Academy Awards, including Best Director and Best Picture.

Thurgood Marshall (1908–1993), a Baltimore native, was the first African American to serve as a justice on the U.S. Supreme Court. During the 1940s and 1950s, Marshall was the nation's preeminent civil rights lawyer, winning twenty-nine of thirty-two cases that he argued before the Supreme Court. In his most famous case, *Brown v. Board of Education of Topeka, Kansas*, the court agreed with his position and declared the segregation (racial separation) of public schools illegal. Marshall served on the Supreme Court from 1967 to 1991.

H. L. Mencken (1880–1956) was a journalist and social critic whose columns poked fun at politics, religion, and middle-class values. Mencken became a reporter for the *Baltimore Morning Herald* at age eighteen. By age twenty-five, he had become the paper's editor in chief. He later moved to the *Baltimore Sun*. Mencken also shaped public opinion and literary tastes as a writer and editor of such sophisticated magazines as *Smart Set* and *American Mercury*. He was born in Baltimore.

Barbara Mikulski (1936–) was the first female U.S. senator from Maryland, the first Democratic woman to hold a U.S. Senate seat not previously held by her husband, and the first woman to win a statewide election in Maryland. Mikulski grew up in Baltimore and became a social worker. In 1971, she was elected to the Baltimore City Council. She moved to the U.S. House of Representatives in 1977 and then to the Senate ten years later. Mikulski is known for her feisty liberal and feminist views. She remains in the Senate today.

Barbara Mikulski

Phyllis Reynolds Naylor (1933–) has written many acclaimed books for young people. She is best known for her books about serious subjects, such as *The Keeper*, which concerns mental illness. However, she has also written lighthearted mysteries such as *The Agony of Alice*. Her 1992 novel *Shiloh*, which involves an abused dog, won the prestigious Newbery Award for children's literature. Naylor lives in Bethesda.

Charles Willson Peale (1741–1827), one of the leading American painters of his age, was born in Queen Anne's County. The first artist to paint George Washington, Peale made his reputation as a portraitist. He established the oldest art school in the country, the Pennsylvania Academy of Fine Arts. He also founded the Peale Museum, which was the first scientific museum in the United States. It housed live reptiles, fish, toads, and larger animals. It even held an entire mastodon skeleton that Peale had helped excavate. His most famous painting, *The Exhumation of the Mastodon*, documents this event.

Adrienne Rich (1929–), a native of Baltimore, is a leading poet whose work reflects her commitment to feminism and social change. Her 1966 poetry collection *Necessities of Life* won the National Book Award.

Cal Ripken Jr. (1960–), of Havre de Grace, is one of the best all-round shortstops in baseball history. Ripken, who spent his entire career with the Baltimore Orioles, holds the record for the most consecutive games played, at 2,632. He also won the American League Most Valuable Player Award twice and has more career home runs than any other American League shortstop.

Cal Ripken Jr.

George Herman "Babe" Ruth (1895–1948), one of the greatest players in baseball history, was born in Baltimore. For many years he held the record for most home runs in a single season. His record of 714 career home runs stood until 1974. Ruth was one of the first five players elected to the National Baseball Hall of Fame.

Upton Sinclair (1878–1968) was a writer and social critic best remembered for his novel *The Jungle*, which exposed the filthy conditions and unfair labor practices of the meatpacking industry. The outcry that resulted from his book provoked the passage of the Pure Food and Drug Law. Sinclair wrote more than ninety other books, many of which dealt with corruption and unsafe practices in industry. Sinclair was born in Baltimore.

Harriet Tubman (1820–1913) was a leading figure in the Underground Railroad, which helped escaped slaves make their way to freedom in the North. Tubman, who was born a slave in Bucktown, escaped north in 1848. During the following ten years, she made many trips south to help others escape—including her parents. During the Civil War, Tubman worked as a nurse, a spy, and a scout for the Union Army. After the war, she advocated for women's rights and established a home for elderly and needy African Americans.

Anne Tyler (1941–   ), who lives in Baltimore, is an acclaimed novelist. Her works, such as *The Accidental Tourist* and *Dinner at the Homesick Restaurant*, are noted for their mix of comedy and drama. In 1989, her novel *Breathing Lessons* won the Pulitzer Prize for fiction.

Frank Zappa (1940–1993) was a groundbreaking rock musician and an accomplished composer. Zappa's songs ranged from jazz to rock to modern classical. He often used montage techniques that interwove rock and orchestral music with spoken words and bursts of noise. His more than sixty albums, including *We're Only in It for the Money* and *Weasels Ripped My Flesh*, feature satirical songs with sharp political criticism. Zappa was born in Baltimore.

TOUR THE STATE

Antietam National Battlefield (Sharpsburg) Tour the bloodiest battlefield of the Civil War and visit the cemetery where nearly four thousand soldiers are buried. Then stop at the visitor's center and learn about how the battle turned the tide of the war in favor of the Union.

Western Maryland Scenic Railroad (Cumberland) This 1916 locomotive takes visitors on a 32-mile trip through the lovely Allegheny Mountains.

Western Maryland Scenic Railroad

Havre de Grace Decoy Museum (Havre de Grace) This unusual museum is filled with 1,500 decoys shaped like ducks, geese, and swans. On weekends you can watch craftspeople demonstrate the art of carving decoys.

Swallow Falls State Park (Oakland) Trails along the rugged Youghiogheny River take hikers past rocky gorges to a stunning waterfall. The park is also a great place to fish and to camp.

Fort McHenry National Monument and Shrine (Baltimore) Today this star-shaped fort, which was finished in 1803, looks much like it did during the Civil War. You can tour restored guardrooms and barracks, examine early-American weapons, and sometimes even watch reenactments of life at the fort during the nineteenth century.

Baltimore Streetcar Museum (Baltimore) Hop on a restored streetcar for a 1.25-mile ride into yesteryear. Many other streetcars, dating back as far as 1859, are also on display.

National Aquarium (Baltimore) More than five thousand fish, sharks, dolphins, reptiles, birds, and other creatures live at this aquarium, the most visited tourist site in Baltimore. Highlights include the coral reef exhibit, the shark tank, and the rain forest exhibit.

American Visionary Art Museum (Baltimore) This fascinating museum displays works by artists who taught themselves, including farmers, housewives, disabled people, and homeless people. Some of the paintings and sculptures are made from unusual materials such as toothpicks and household utensils.

Babe Ruth Birthplace and Baseball Center (Baltimore) The man widely believed to be one of the greatest baseball players ever was born in this brick row house. Today the house is filled with photos, film clips, and memorabilia of Ruth and other great Baltimore baseball players.

Maryland State House (Annapolis) First occupied in 1780, this is the oldest state capitol to be continuously used by a legislature. The building's intricate woodwork and wooden dome are particularly striking.

NASA/Goddard Visitor Center and Museum (Greenbelt) This museum provides visitors with a close-up view of satellites, rockets, and space capsules. You might even see a model rocket launch.

Spruce Forest Artisan Village (Grantsville) Potters, weavers, stained-glass makers, and other artisans create their crafts in this village's nineteenth-century log buildings.

Calvert Cliffs State Park (Lusby) More than six hundred kinds of fossils, some fifteen million years old, have been found embedded in the Calvert Cliffs, which tower above Chesapeake Bay. Visitors can scour the beach looking for shark's teeth and other fossils. Any fossils they find are theirs to keep.

Historic St. Mary's City (Lexington Park) You can journey back to colonial times when you visit the site of the first European settlement in Maryland. The museum includes the reconstructed state house, which was first built in 1676. It exhibits a replica of the *Dove*, a boat that brought the first European settlers to colonial Maryland. At the Godiah Spray Tobacco Plantation, costumed guides tell of life in the seventeenth century.

Battle Creek Cypress Swamp Sanctuary (Prince Frederick) This sanctuary has the northernmost stand of towering bald cypress trees in the United States. A boardwalk that winds through the swamp gives you a close-up view of the native plants and animals.

Blackwater National Wildlife Refuge (Cambridge) Bald eagles, ospreys, Canada geese, peregrine falcons, Delmarva fox squirrels, and many other creatures live in this refuge. Hiking trails provide visitors with a view of the region's woodlands, marshes, ponds, and other habitats.

Assateague Island National Seashore (Assateague Island) This pristine island is ideal for camping, hiking, fishing, and picnicking. Keep an eye out for the wild ponies that roam the island.

Chesapeake Bay Maritime Museum (St. Michaels) Displays of boats, ranging from skipjacks to Indian dugout canoes, are just one highlight of this museum. There are also exhibits about fishing, navigation, and boatbuilding; an aquarium; and a six-sided lighthouse built in 1879.

Ward Museum of Wildfowl Art (Salisbury) The history of decoys is brought to life at this museum. Displays range from replicas of the reed figures Native Americans made a thousand years ago to intricate contemporary carvings worth hundreds of thousands of dollars.

FUN FACTS

Baltimore is the site of the nation's first umbrella factory. The company's slogan was "Born in Baltimore—raised everywhere."

Maryland was the first state to adopt a shield law, which protects reporters from being required to reveal their sources.

In 1905, Mary Titcomb, a librarian at the Washington County Free Library, implemented her idea for a traveling library. This is now known as a bookmobile.

The first practical refrigerator was invented in Baltimore in 1803.

Baltimore is also the site of many other firsts. Peter Cooper built the country's first coal-burning steam engine for the Baltimore and Ohio Railroad in 1830. The nation's first telegraph began operation in 1844 between Baltimore and Washington, D.C. The country's first elevated electric railway was built in Baltimore in 1893.

The SCR-270, considered to be the first operational radar in the United States, was built in Baltimore between 1941 and 1943.

America's first investment banking house, Alexander Brown and Sons, was opened in Baltimore in 1800.

The first dental college in the world, the Baltimore College of Dental Surgery, was founded in 1840.

Baltimore's football team, the Ravens, and its baseball team, the Orioles, have something in common. Before moving to Baltimore in 1996, the Ravens were named the Browns. Before the Orioles moved to Baltimore in 1954, they also were called the Browns.

Find Out More

If you would like to find out more about Maryland, look in your school library, local library, bookstore, or video store. You can also surf the Internet. Here are some resources to help you begin your search.

BOOKS

Marsh, Carole. *Maryland History Projects: 30 Cool Activities, Crafts, Experiments & More for Kids to Do to Learn About Your State*. Peachtree City, GA: Gallopade International, 2003.

Otis, James. *Calvert of Maryland: A Story of Lord Baltimore's Colony*. Whitefish, MT: Kessinger Publishing, 2005.

Somervill, Barbara A. *Maryland*. New York: Children's Press, 2003.

Sonneborn, Liz. *A Primary Source History of the Colony of Maryland*. New York: Rosen Central Publishing, 2005.

VIDEOS

Bike-O-Vision Journey #9: Washington D.C., Historic Virginia & Maryland. Rockstone Productions, 2005.

Biography: Frederick Douglass. A&E Home Video, 2005.

Discoveries . . . America: Maryland. Bennett-Watt Entertainment, Inc., 2005.

WEB SITES

Maryland.gov

http://www.maryland.gov

At Maryland's official Web site, you can learn about the state's history, find out about fun tourist attractions and outdoor activities, and read an overview of state and local governments.

The Maryland Kids Page

http://www.mdkidspage.org/

Explore Maryland's lighthouses or download a flag to color on your own.

The Maryland Science Center

http://www.mdsci.org/

Learn how you can visit and participate in hands-on science projects at this museum.

Index

Page numbers in **boldface** are illustrations and charts.

ABOUT THE AUTHORS

Leslie Pietrzyk is a writer who lives in Alexandria, Virginia—about a five-minute drive across the Potomac River to Maryland. She works at an area chamber of commerce. When she can't decide whether to eat Maryland steamed crabs or Maryland crab cakes, she has both! She is a die-hard Baltimore Orioles Fan.

Martha Kneib is a native St. Louisan who has published two historical novels, several short stories, and nonfiction works. Martha earned degrees in anthropology from the University of Tulsa and Kent State University. She has worked both in the field, at Keystone Lake in Oklahoma, and in the lab as a graduate assistant. Currently, she serves on the faculty of Webster University in St. Louis. The Kneib household includes Martha, her husband, a multitude of pet rats, and three cats.